They have many names—
Healthy Happy Holy Organization
Intercosmic Center of Spiritual Association
Church of World Messianity-Johrei
Bishop Devernon DeGrand's Church
Dawn House Communion
The Church of Armageddon
Self-Realization Fellowship
Brother Julius' Followers
Erhard Seminar Training (est)
Transcendental Meditation
Integral Yoga Institute
Divine Light Mission
The Unification Church
Holy Order of Mans

Inner Light Foundation
Children of God
The Way International
Zen Buddhism
The Baba Lovers
Hare Krishna
Soka Gakkai
The Local Church
The Church, The Body,
Scientology, Eckankar,
Satanism, Bahai,
Subud

They have one goal—
to take over the lives and minds of young people (and adults)

They are—
the youthnappers

P9-CQK-945

The Youthnappers

James C. Hefley

VICTOR BOOKS

a division of SP Publications, Inc., Wheaton, Illinois
Offices also in Fullerton, California • Whitby, Ontario, Canada • London, England

Library of Congress Catalog Card Number: 77-79356
ISBN: 0-88207-754-6

© 1977 by SP Publications, Inc. World rights reserved
Printed in the United States of America

VICTOR BOOKS
A division of SP Publications, Inc.
P.O. Box 1825 • Wheaton, Ill. 60187

Contents

105319

1

The New Cults Are Here!

New York City: Cadres of neat coveralled youth march in Wall Street. Hundreds of young, clean-cut whites wielding brooms sweep the streets of Harlem, singing as they go. Big red, white, and blue posters all around the city announce a giant "Bicentennial God Bless America Rally" in Yankee Stadium featuring Sun Myung Moon.

The operation is backed by more money and enthusiasm than Billy Graham could ever muster for a one-shot crusade.

Los Angeles: Seven weeks later, the International Society of Krishna Consciousness (Hare Krishna) celebrates the 5,000th birthday of their "supreme godhead" with a lavish display outdoing even Hollywood. Costumed youth feast, dance, and chant before Lord Krishna's bathed-in-nectar seven-foot-high image. In an ancient fire ceremony, grains and fruits are offered to the deity. There is a butter-churning contest, as well as movies, lectures, art exhibits, and a puppet show. Then comes the grand finale: a thousand "faithful" sitting down to a multi-layered, splendidly-lit 600-pound cake topped with five nectar fountains and four, large, simulated elephants.

All to the glory and honor of Lord Krishna whose saried and pigtailed followers are dancing across America.

The new cults are not just in New York and Los Angeles, where people would hardly look up if a real UFO landed. They're in the heartland between.

Houston: The teenage "Lord of the Universe", Guru Maharaj Ji, and his Divine Light Mission rent the Astrodome for what they said would be the "most significant event in the history of humanity" (it wasn't).

St. Petersburg: Scientology purchases the historic Fort Harrison Hotel to be its "Flag Land Base" for training international leaders.

New Knoxville, Ohio: Victor Paul Wierwille puts down "roots" for the worldwide spread of his new revelation, lost since apostolic times, that Jesus is *not* God.

Seattle: Love Israel, a strange man with hypnotic power and a long arrest record, who has "freed" his love slaves from fears of using chemicals, rules the Church of Armageddon.

Fairfield, Iowa: Maharishi Mahesh Yogi, the guru of Transcendental Meditation opens his Maharishi International University (on a former Presbyterian campus) to train TM leaders for reaching the world's four billion people.

On and on it goes. In cities and rural areas across the United States, Canada, and Western Europe, strange extensions of Hinduism, Buddhism, and ancient Gnosticism, along with newly revived "Christian" heresies, are pouring into the spiritual vacuum of the West.

These groups are buying up campuses and church buildings abandoned by shrinking Christian denominations. They are utilizing the tools of modern communications and promotion, franchising local operations *à la* Colonel Sanders, and recruiting young people brought up in Protestant, Catholic, and Jewish families, and those with no religious affiliation.

Hundreds of thousands of Americans have become involved with the new cults. University of Chicago anthropologist Irving Zaretsky estimates from his 10-year study that 20 million, perhaps even more, have some involvement in "fringe religious cults."

The most active, militant members are young people from 18 to 26. They come from both religious and irreligious family backgrounds, from poor and wealthy homes, from illiterate and intellectual parentage.

The bewildering success of the cults has engendered bitter charges and counterclaims. Parents' groups, organized to free young people from "enslaving" cultic leaders, allege brainwashing, fraud, deception, and other gross violations of law and human dignity. Leaders of the new religions deny wrongdoing and say they are only evangelizing and indoctrinating, as the establishment churches have been doing all along. Their opponents, they say, are guilty of "kidnapping" and "deprogramming" young people out of freely chosen faiths. There have been suits and countersuits, sometimes within families.

The controversy has spilled over into legislatures, the mental health profession, the news media, and church councils.

Take only two contrasting views about what should be done about Sun Myung Moon's Unification Church, the biggest newsmaker.

Rev. Richard John Newhaus, a Missouri Synod Lutheran pastor, has cautioned coolness. Christians who join the hunt may find themselves "blown up by their own petard," he warned in the inter-Lutheran monthly *Forum* publication (July, 1976):

> Of course Moon's theology is anti-Christian; of course his politics are odious; of course his methods are bizarre . . . but many who are savaging Moon now clearly have at heart an animosity toward any religious phenomenon that doesn't accommodate to their secular worldviews. . . . Instead of running with the hounds after Moon, Christians should be protecting him from government regulation that is finally an assault upon all of us. Defending the unsavory is sometimes necessary to saving the more defensible.

But Dr. George Swope, an American Baptist minister and leader among the parent groups, said:

> Members of my family, my ancestors, have died that men might be atheists or agnostics or Christians or Jews or Moslems or whatever else. I have wrestled with the question before us today: When should there be careful investigation of a nonreligious ideology that uses the terminology of religion and is basically subversive to our government, destructive of our homes, and is channeling the creative potential of wonderful young people into drab and nonproductive morasses?

Swope concluded that the Moon organization

"should be investigated by several agencies of government—perhaps, by Congress itself—and exposed as the nonreligious, personality-destroying danger to America it is."

With the battle lines so drawn, there is, first, a critical need for calm, rational examination of the controversial groups—their origins, beliefs, leadership, methods, and goals. Do they really "brainwash" and alienate young people from their parents? Or is their indoctrination basically the same as practiced by more acceptable religious groups?

Second, it is important to examine the attempts being made by aggrieved parents and other opponents to "rescue" young people from cults. Do parents have a right to kidnap their own children for deprogramming? Is deprogramming a violation of human rights? What else can be done to combat the cults?

Third, it is necessary to consider what has happened in American life to make so many youths receptive to beliefs and practices inimical to their upbringing.

We will try to answer these and other crucial questions as fairly and as objectively as possible in the following chapters.

2

New Moon Rising

Sun Myung Moon rose in the American sky, beaming and brilliant, over the dark cloud of Watergate in the fall of 1973. He had come before without being noticed. This time people could hardly miss the round, placid Oriental face, which his Great American Public-Relations Machine had plastered on posters and full-page newspaper ads, or the big, black lettering:

CHRISTIANITY IN CRISIS
NEW HOPE
REV. SUN MYUNG MOON

Moon kicked off his 21-city Day of Hope Tour with a banquet for VIPs in New York's Waldorf Astoria.

Beribboned generals and black-tied city fathers praised him as a great anti-Communist Christian leader who had come to spark a revival of morality and patriotism. His goals, he said, were no less than to make America into the truly Christian nation the founders had intended, to unify all mankind, and to bring in the kingdom of God on earth. He was dusting off the dream of the earthly millenial kingdom that had fired Protestants in the 19th century.

They loved him in New York and in the 20 other cities on the tour. Always he was preceded by squads of freshly scrubbed, pink-cheeked young Americans, marching against pornography, cleaning up dirty streets, singing patriotic songs, and brightening the spirits of shoppers with their smiles. Then Moon would jet in, like a visiting prime minister, to speak to local leadership at a free banquet in the city's most posh ballroom and afterward address a public rally in a large, crowded auditorium.

Reporters and others curious about Moon's background were given copies of a crisply written official biography, describing his rise to prominence as follows:

1. Born into a North Korean family of eight children, he early had a "strong desire to live a life of high dimension," and at 12 "asked for wisdom greater than Solomon's."

2. "On Easter morning of 1936, Jesus appeared to him to talk about his future life." It was "God's desire to establish His kingdom on earth. Reverend Moon was asked to assume the responsibility."

3. Over the next nine years, Moon received the divine revelation "progressively through prayer, study of all religious scriptures, meditation . . . and direct communication with God. . . . Led by God to solve a vast spiritual puzzle, [he] was now ready to bring this revelation to the world."

4. Moon put aside his vocation of electrical engineering to launch his public ministry in North Korea, where the Communist government had him

arrested, tortured, and beaten, before he was freed by a United Nations landing force.

5. Moon officially formed the Unification Church (UC) in 1954 and three years later published his revelations in a book called *Divine Principle*. By 1955 the "foundation for the Korean Church was sufficiently enough established" to allow him to launch "his broader mission" in 40 nations. He came to America following "God's call," believing that the salvation of the world depended on this country.

Press agents for such luminaries as Ted Kennedy and Hubert Humphrey fell over themselves getting their bosses' pictures taken with Moon and his American aides. In Georgia, then Governor Jimmy Carter signed on November 1, 1973 a five-paragraph "Day of Hope and Unification" statement in honor of Moon's visit to America. Carter lauded Moon as one who "has dedicated his life to increasing the worldwide understanding of hope and unity under God."

Moon's biggest public-relations push came from embattled Richard Nixon. Twelve hundred of the Korean's clean-cut young followers turned up at the national Christmas tree lighting ceremony at the White House in December. They carried signs proclaiming, "God loves Nixon," and "Support the President." As Nixon came to thank them in LaFayette Park, some knelt before him.

Moon's Watergate strategy was a public-relations stroke of genius for gaining sympathy and national attention. He sermonized that the solution to Watergate was for America to forgive, love, and unite. The message was inserted into the Congressional Record four days before Christmas.

Five weeks later Moon beamed at the National Prayer Breakfast in the Washington Hilton, while outside a thousand of his disciples sang patriotic songs and whooped up support for Nixon. The next day Nixon invited him to the White House, where they reportedly embraced; then Moon "prayed fervently in his native tongue while the President listened in silence."

When Nixon resigned in August, young Moonies massed in front of the White House to burn candles and sing hymns.

Nixon faded away while Sun Myung Moon kept rising. By summer's end 1974, he had spoken in all 50 states. His Unification Church held title to a complex of expensive properties in the Hudson River Valley: an $850,000 estate for use as a training center; a $1.5 million seminary purchased from the Catholics; a $625,000 mansion for Moon and his family, along with a couple of yachts for their sailing pleasure. Most important, hundreds of the country's brightest and best young people had left all to follow him.

Buoyed by a Freedoms Foundation Award, Moon launched in the fall of 1974 an even bigger "Day of Hope" nationwide campaign. His Washington banquet, for example, drew 3,000 high level leaders—congressmen, ambassadors, Pentagon brass, church leaders, even prophetess Jeane Dixon. Neil Salonen, president of the American branch of Moon's church, a Dale Carnegie graduate and director of a psychiatric hospital before joining Moon, cited the impressive programs of various Unification Church fronts (though he didn't call them that):

The Freedom Leadership Foundation was fighting the "radical left" on campuses and publishing a weekly anti-Communist newspaper, *The Rising Tide.*

The D.C. Striders Track Club was developing the talents of inner-city blacks. Members already held six world records, Salonen bragged.

The Collegiate Association for the Research of Principles was leading students "to a life of high morality and responsible citizenship."

The International Cultural Foundation was "promoting cultural and academic studies directed toward world peace." ICF performing groups included world-famous singers, dancers, and musicians.

Then Salonen introduced the star of the evening. Resplendent in a dark blue suit and red-striped silk tie, Moon spoke in gutteral Korean, interpreted by his aide, Colonel Bo Hi Pak. "Parents are for children and children for parents, employers for employees, and employees for employers," he said. "America was for God and God was for America. Selflessness must reign over selfishness, humility over pride." Bland, comfortable clichés with which everyone could agree.

After a public "rebirthday" rally in Constitution Square, the bandwagon rolled on to other cities.

Here and there a few dissidents shouted questions about Moon's finances, but were hissed down. A few church people carried Scripture signs around parking lots warning that Moon might be a "false Christ." Moon's entourage passed them off as sincere objectors who didn't understand.

Unfortunately for Moon, the big media now had his scent. Reporters dogged Moon, Salonen, and other leaders, asking about church properties, fund-raising, beliefs, political ties, and recruiting and training methods. And was it true that young Moonies had been brainwashed and turned into smiling zombies, as some parents were charging?

Moon and his Unification Church never broke stride. Through 1975 and into the Bicentennial year they bought full-page ads in the largest newspapers to publish Moon's sermons and answer "false" charges. As exposés by defectors rolled off presses, the Unification Church kept spending more money for banquets and rallies, and buying more real estate for expansion in major cities. In New York the church purchased the towering 2,200-room New Yorker Hotel and the imposing Columbia Club near Fifth Avenue.

Moon was now going to speak to Congress, his promoters announced.

He actually spoke at a breakfast in the House Caucus Room by the courtesy of Rep. Bill Chappell, Jr. of Florida. Any congressman could reserve the room, and Chappell acted at the request of Unification Church members. He was neither "a believer or disbeliever in Moon." Only four other Congressmen attended, though invitations had been sent to every House and Senate member.

Rep. Richard Ichord, a veteran anti-Communist fighter, introduced Moon, calling him "a man of God and a positive force for good in the world." The controversy surrounding Moon and the Unification Church was natural, he said. "Most of the great religious movements of the past have stirred religious controversy. And so have the great religious leaders, one being our Lord Jesus Christ."

Moon repeated that America had been chosen by God to receive the Messiah and that the Unification Church was destined to play a major role in establishing the messianic kingdom. Then unexpectedly he responded to the brainwashing charges.

"Are Americans really that foolish? Can they really be brainwashed by Reverend Moon, a Korean? I know your answer is no. . . . No American is so foolish."

Moon declined to comment on stories circulating about his past—stories that differed from the version his promoters were pushing. The anti-Moon claims were:

1. Moon had borrowed much of his doctrine from the Israel Soodo Won (Israel Monastery), which he once led as the sinless Lord of the Second Advent. The Monastery had practiced a strange rite called "blood cleansing" in which women had sexual intercourse with the leader and men had intercourse with women so cleansed.

2. Moon had changed his original name of Yong (meaning dragon) Myung Moon to Sun Myung Moon. With Myung meaning "shining," he became to Koreans "Shining Sun and Moon," a suggestion of cosmic divinity.

3. Moon's imprisonment in North Korea was for bigamy and adultery. He had not launched his anti-Communist campaign till 1962, years after he left North Korea.

4. Moon had been excommunicated by the Presbyterian Church of Korea in 1948.

5. *Divine Principle* had actually been written by a dropout medical student named Hye Won Yoo and then been passed off as Moon's.

6. In 1954 Moon's second wife left him because she could not comprehend his mission. The following year, he and several followers were arrested by

Seoul police for draft-dodging, adultery, and pro-
miscuity. But Moon was acquitted and claimed
persecution.

7. In 1960 Moon married his present wife, then
an 18-year-old high school graduate.

Stories also began spreading that Moon's young
operatives were attempting to influence federal
legislation. Columnist Jack Anderson reported that
the attractive, hazel-eyed girl seen frequently in
House Speaker Carl Albert's company was Susan
Bergman, a Moon disciple. And that a gold-
trimmed copy of Moon's *Divine Principle* was
among Albert's reference books. Albert explained
that Miss Bergman was just a "very nice Jewish girl
who got all hepped up on the Lord Jesus . . . and
is trying to convert me." Albert also denied any
impropriety with other suspected Moon girls seen
accompanying him on trips.

The big blow came in February 1976 when over
300 ex-cultists, government officials, and press
crowded into a Senate caucus room for a "Day of
Affirmation and Protest" against the Unification
Church and other fast-growing cults.

An ad hoc national committee of representatives
from various parents' groups protested "the destruc-
tive cults and their strategy of alienation—the
alienation of psychologically kidnapped youth from
their government, families, prior religions, education, society and its viable values."

The testimonies of parents and ex-cultists
(mostly former Moonies) were front-paged across
the country and darkened the shadow over Moonism.

Nevertheless, Moon's church went ahead with
June bicentennial extravaganzas in Yankee Stadium

and at the Washington Monument. Moon reportedly spent a million dollars promoting the Yankee Stadium rally that was dampened by a thunderstorm and drew less than 50,000 people. While Moon was speaking, hundreds of demonstrators outside carried such signs as, "Don't Settle for Moonshine," and "Jesus Christ is Lord, not Mr. Moon." Disturbances also flared inside the stadium, but Moon was undeterred and declared that "the world's greatest religion" (the Unification Church) was in fact "taking up where Judaism and Christianity had failed to bring about God's kingdom on earth."

A few weeks later the U.S. Immigration Department delivered Moon another setback, ordering deportation of some 700 Moonies to Korea and Japan on grounds they had not been doing the missionary work claimed on their visas.

The Washington Monument rally in September was another disappointment. The UC claimed 300,000 attended; the National Park Service estimated only 50,000.

More mysteries of Moonism are now coming to light. His *Divine Principle* is being scrutinized by theologians. Former members are telling what life is like in the Moon family. "Inside" training documents, smuggled out by ex-Moonies, reveal hitherto unknown teachings.

In the remainder of this chapter, we will consider nine key aspects of what is now known about Moon and his Unification Church.

1. *Moon's doctrine* Moon's theology hangs on three "Adams." The first Adam failed in Eden to establish God's kingdom on earth. The second Adam, Jesus, failed when He was crucified. The

third Adam, the "Lord of the Second Advent," will succeed.

Moon's account of the episode in Eden differs from the biblical record. Eve was first seduced by Lucifer and bore Cain, the portent of mankind's relationship with Satan. Then from Eve's legitimate union with Adam came Abel, the symbol of mankind's relationship with God.

History is the conflict between these two forces, with God trying to defeat Satan by eradicating the Cain strain through a spiritual and physical redemption. Noah, Abraham, David, and other divinely appointed leaders tried valiantly without succeeding. Then a perfect Man was born, Jesus. But again, God's purpose was thwarted when this Second Adam was "invaded by Satan" and crucified. Had Jesus not died, Moon speculates, He might have found a mate and established the perfect family that God had intended before the fall. As it happened, His death provided only for man's spiritual salvation.

Jesus' failure set the stage for the coming of the Lord of the Second Advent, Third Adam, who would be born in Korea, separate himself from Satan and the Cain strain by paying an indemnity, and establish the perfect Family for bringing in God's kingdom on earth.

Moon has never publicly identified himself as Third Adam, though many of his followers believe he is this messiah. "In the beginning we prayed to God," ex-Moonie Arthur Robbins recalls. "But eventually we were told to end our prayers 'in the name of our true parents, Moon and Mother Moon!'"

Some of Moon's statements from his "Master

Speaks" series of talks suggest he is just short of making the formal announcement that he is messiah.

"From now on, the work of restoration will be speeded up because the True Parents are now on earth. God can now lead you through them" (March and April 1965).

"No one else but Master can do this (save the world) . . . So, in that sense I am the foremost one in the whole world" (November 1974).

"We have worked barely less than three years in New York. But has there ever been such a person who has become so well-known in less than three years' time . . . ?" (August 1974)

Similar broad hints have been given by Moon's training director, Ken Sudo, to new members:

"You are not American anymore, you are . . . humankind centering in True Parents. As an example of the way of life we have no example but the True Parents. We have no way of life or how to love except by True Parents . . . (Father) Moon is the beginning of a new mankind . . ."

2. *Sex and Marriage* Moon wants his faithful followers to marry and build up the Perfect Family. To emphasize the importance of marriage, he has conducted two mass marriages that made world headlines. In Seoul, October 1970 he presided at the wedding of 791 couples from 10 countries. In 1975, he more than doubled this record, marrying 1,800 couples in an all-day celebration in the Korean capital.

Moon expects chastity before marriage. His single "children" may not hold hands during a lecture or even sit next to the opposite sex. "Before you are blessed (married) you must be like a blossom shut tight, and bear the fragrance deep within you," he has warned.

Moonies must prove themselves in faithfu¹ service before they can be "blessed." They may present a choice of mates, but final decisions are made by Moon and his top leaders. Couples who have not even known one another previously may be paired. Before marriage, all must confess any previous sexual sins to an approved representative of Father Moon.

Newlyweds must continue to be celibate until they reach a desired level of spiritual perfection. This may take from 40 days to three years. Even after their union is consummated, they are expected to live more as brothers and sisters in the Family than as husbands and wives.

3. *Public Relations* Big banquets and rallies are staged primarily to build influence and a favorable public image. Events sponsored by front organizations are for the same purpose.

The International Cultural Foundation, one of over 40 Moon fronts operating in the U.S., has sponsored four annual international conferences on the Unity of the Sciences. The first three, featuring some of the biggest names in science, ran smoothly. The fourth encountered rough seas after the Foundation was publicly exposed as a Moon front.

Scheduled for four days at the Waldorf Astoria Hotel, the avowed purpose of the conference was to bring together "the world's most eminent scholars and scientists to reflect on the nature of scientific knowledge and to discuss the relation of science to a standard of value."

A "Who's Who" of scientists, including several Nobel Prize winners, the president of a Presbyterian seminary, and a former presidential science adviser, agreed to staff the program. Honorariums of around $3,000 were promised to each major speaker.

A few weeks before the conference was to open, the participants received a disquieting letter from Daphne Green, chairman of the board of the Graduate Theological Union in Berkeley, California. Having two children in the Unification Church, she knew something about the sponsors, and what she shared in her letter was not good. Many responded that they either had not known of the Moon connection or were unfamiliar with his past. The program roster was gutted by dropouts. However, the conference went on, with all expenses paid by the Moon front.

4. *Member Recruitment* Typically, young people respond first to some "front" appeal—perhaps a dinner, lecture, weekend workshop, or ad in the newspaper for "Peace Corps" type work. They usually don't know what they're getting into, as illustrated by this case history.

John Spradling, then studying piano in Vienna, Austria:

I was leaving a concert hall when a fellow blocked my path and asked if I thought the stabilization of the family structure could save the world. I was interested in that idea and had discussed it with my mother a lot. As a teacher's aide in a depressed area, she runs across children all the time who are victims of separated and divorced parents. So I agreed to meet with him and discuss the question. Then after a few sessions he invited me to a weekend workshop. Because he assured me it was a Christian group, I saw no harm in going. From the workshop I went on for more training until I reached the point where I could accept the doctrine of Moon.

5. *Member Training* "Babes" (new members) are run through progressive 7-, 21-, 40-, and 120-day intensive training sessions. "We do not brainwash," Neil Salonen insisted at a Washington press conference. "We just expect a high level of dedication."

Several newspaper reporters who have infiltrated Moonie training sessions disagree. The *National Enquirer's* Malcolm Boyes, for example, "escaped" to tell of days and nights of "the most intense indoctrination—a torturous regimen of chanting, singing, shouting, praying, and relentless brainwashing" that pushed him to the breaking point. "I feared that if I remained one day longer I might succumb to this crazy mental pressure cooker."

Cynthia Slaughter, a former Fort Worth debutante, who since leaving the Unification Church has become one of its most vociferous opponents, describes her conditioning as follows:

During the [initial] weekend [workshop], which could be compared to a "sorority rush," I was coerced into staying through fear and guilt. I joined The Family after attending a seven-day training session in Noble, Oklahoma. During that time I was never left alone and the days were filled with constant singing, praying, working, and hearing lectures. After I returned to the Boulder (Colorado) center, I had a schedule of fund-raising at street corners and in businesses for 14-16 hours a day. There was constant singing and praying, and I was very fatigued all of the time. I frequently took cold showers, which were supposed to drive out evil spirits, and I sprinkled holy salt on my food and bed to ward off evil spirits. After three weeks in the movement, I did not know what day it was [from one day] to the next and my only concern was overcoming Satan. Satan had become anything that disagreed with my belief or anyone who tried to take me out of the movement.

Some say brainwashing is too strong a term for the indoctrination. "I think the media has blown it out of proportion," says John Spradling, who left voluntarily "without coercion from anyone outside. I admit that I was deceived, but I don't think I ever lost my power of choice."

6. *Fund raising* A "babe" is expected to give up everything when he joins. If he has a car or savings at home, an older member accompanies him to close up accounts. One babe reportedly gave $300,000 from the sale of stock.

After training, the new Moonie may be assigned to one of the many fund-raising teams that criss-cross the country. Each team carries a bound volume of glowing letters and endorsements collected from naive pastors and public officials. Using the book, they get fund-raising permits, if possible, and solicit donations for flowers, candles, gum, and other things in public places. Using the name of a church front, they ask for money to fight drug abuse, pornography or some other social evil. According to many former members, they are told it is "all right to lie for God, because it's Satan's world anyway."

Everything goes to the church except for minimal

room and board. When the leadership announced the need for $280,000 to make a down payment on the Belvedere Estate in New York for a training center, all members dropped everything else and did nothing but raise funds for eight weeks. They reportedly raised the down payment and more.

The Unification Church hedges about full disclosure of income. *Newsweek* estimated gross income of $12 million in the U.S. during 1975.

7. *Properties* The value of UC properties in New York State alone is affixed at $17 million. In Washington, D.C. the Moon empire owns 44 percent of the New Diplomat National Bank. In Oklahoma the church purchased an ice-cream store for $20,000 and a farm for $235,000. Other businesses and houses are owned in various parts of the country.

Moon himself has five Korean companies that manufacture arms, machinery, paint, stone handicrafts, and ginseng tea. The latter is marketed through hundreds of stores in the U.S.; you can buy it at Sears' health shops. Moon also has factories in Japan.

Just how much is Moon and the Unification Church worth? One estimate conservatively puts the figure at $75 million. This helps explain how a million dollars can be made available to promote one rally. And how Moon himself can live in baronial splendor.

8. *Members and their Parents* Church information director W. Farley Jones insists children are not taught "to hate their parents. This is not at all our position . . . In fact, the opposite is true—we encourage love in all relationships. This is why most members grow close to their families."

Paul Engel of Westchester County, New York told a much different story at the Day of Affirmation and Protest:

> After three weeks of continuous indoctrination . . . I was confronted with a situation where my mother was ill and my father had called. . . . Before I was allowed to speak to him, my group leader talked with me for about 10 or 15 minutes, explaining the reason for my mother's sickness. She told me that Satan had invaded her and it was because Satan was working through my family. . . . Therefore, I was asked to go against my own emotions toward my family. And she actually told me what to say over the phone. . . .

Scores of parents have tearfully related similar stories from their perspective. Mrs. Donald Dysart of Temple, Texas told the same Washington audience:

> . . . She (our daughter, Sandra) called us to tell us she was quitting school to join the Unification Church and live in The Family. All plans for career and school were to be abandoned. . . . Her letters and phone calls became increasingly disturbed and even when I, her mother, had a mental breakdown and was confined to the hospital she would not or was not allowed to return home. . . .

But you can hear conflicting stories. John Spradling says he wrote his parents every 10 days while in the Unification Church. "If you wish, you can keep good contact. There are kids in the Church whose parents are happy for them to be in." But Spradling concedes that outside phone calls of "select" members, considered shaky in their allegiance, were bugged.

Of course, loyal Moonies take a positive position. Doug Miller, who attended Catholic schools in Kentucky, says he calls his parents every week, has been home several times, and "they feel very positive toward the church."

We have already noted some of the teaching about "family" in the Unification Church. What the Moonies mean by "family" is not what outsiders ordinarily take the word to mean. The True Family is the Unification Church; the True Parents are Moon and his wife. Natural relationships, especially those acquired before joining the church, must be subservient.

Moon's youths are told that their physical parents represent the Satanic Cain position if they oppose the church. Members are to try to bring their loved ones over to the Abel position—in other words, get them into the Unification Church. If this is not possible, they should try to keep on good terms with their families for financial purposes.

At intervals the UC holds carefully staged "parents' days." As Training Director Sudo instructed in a lecture: The "best" food will be served with "beautiful table flowers" and "good entertainment." A "short lecture will be given. . . . They can have questions, and a group leader will serve and solve every question they have. And then they will go back or sign membership."

The biggest parents' day was held at the church's New Yorker Hotel on the weekend before the 1976 rally in Yankee Stadium. George Sheridan, a representative of the Interfaith Department of the Southern Baptist Home Mission Board, happened to be the only nonparent at the carefully orchestrated question-and-answer session. He recalls:

> None of the parents came down hard on anything. The meeting was just a defense for the Unification Church, almost a pep rally with people saying good things and being loudly applauded.
>
> One father stood up and said, "Two of my kids are divorced and miserable. My third kid is in this church and seems very happy." Applause. Another identified himself as a Southern Baptist and said, "We came to see about your church. We see there's a lot of good in it. Can you tell me how I can tithe to it?" Loud applause.
>
> When I would ask a question, people would turn and look at me strangely. One man suggested I was rude and engendering confrontation.
>
> Maybe they were afraid of separating themselves from their kids. One father did tell me in private, "Either I accept my daughter's involvement, or I lose her."

9. *Moon's Politics* Suspicions swirl around Washington that Moon and the Unification Church have links with the Korean government and its CIA.

One finger points at Moon's aide and interpreter, Colonel Bo Hi Pak, who was an assistant military attaché at the Korean Embassy from 1962 to 1964. In 1965 Pak led in founding the Korean Cultural Freedom Foundation ostensibly to foster Korean-American goodwill and finance medical services and other good works in Korea. He later acknowledged that Moon was the "spiritual inspiration." Over a million dollars was raised through mail appeals under a letterhead bearing Washington's most

prestigious names, among them former Presidents
Eisenhower and Truman. Pak remains a director of
the Foundation. About half of the governing board
are Unification Church members.

Moon's maidens are still busy on Capitol Hill.
The *New York Daily News* quoted him as saying in
an "inside" speech, "Master needs many good-
looking girls. We will assign three girls to one Senator. That means we need 300. Let them have a
good relationship with them. If our girls are superior to the Senators in many ways, then the
Senators will be taken in by our members."

Moon presented his religiopolitico goals in an
early training session for U.S. members:

We are going to have an automatic theocracy to
rule the world. . . . We cannot separate the political field from the religious. . . . God-loving people
have to rule the world. . . . We are to purge the
corrupted politicians, and the sons of God must
rule the world. The separation between religion
and politics is what Satan likes most.

But I am not going to send you into the political field right away—but later on when we are
prepared. . . . If we have 500,000 members all
over the country, under one command from
Master, if they are told to come and live in New
York, what would happen? Upon my command
to the Europeans and others throughout the world
to come live in the U.S., wouldn't they obey me?
Then what would happen? We can embrace the
religious world in one arm and the political world
in the other. . . .

The present U.N. must be annihilated by our
power. That is the stage for the Communists. We
must make a new U.N. Then I must be able to

make out of you world-renowned personages. Wouldn't you want to be trained for that? You will have to go through training of such a type that history has never seen.

"I am not a day dreamer," Moon told his followers later. "I am a master tactician or strategist. When I plan, I execute the plan. And when I execute a certain battle plan, I will always come out with a better result than any other tactician in history."

How long does Moon think this will take?

"If you continue (to serve and give unselfishly)," he promised his loyal devotees, "within 20 years the whole world will come under our domain."

Already his Unification Church claims more than two million members in over 120 countries. It is, according to the *Washington Star-News,* "probably the fastest growing faith in the world."

Acclaimed membership is highest in Korea and Japan, with 400,000 and 210,000 respectively. How many has Rev. Shining Sun and Moon netted in the United States? Estimates run to 7,000 live-in members, with another 23,000 regular contributors.

With so much unfavorable publicity and rising pressure for government investigations of Moonism in America, there are indications that Moon is moving his major base of operations to Europe, perhaps to West Germany, where he already claims 6,000 followers.

Even if this happens, Moon's field generals will continue "catching the minds" of thousands of young Americans in his crusade to build a kingdom on earth.

3

Hare Krishna

If the Moonies resemble college squares from the 50s, the exotic youths who seek Krishna-consciousness look like reincarnations from an ancient Hindu temple. Their strange appearance turns eyes: the boys in saffron robes with heads peeled to leave only a single pigtail flopping about; the girls in white saris with cloth purses swinging around their necks. Dancing to drumbeat and tinkling bells, they promenade along sidewalks and airport corridors, offering sandalwood-scented incense and copies of their slick *Back to Godhead* magazine for donations. Always chanting, "Hare Krishna, Hare Krishna, Krishna . . ." Pausing to say softly, "If you can't make a donation, will you please say, 'Hare Krishna'?" Most people do, not realizing the strange words acknowledge Krishna as Lord.

These energized young people belong to the International Society of Krishna Consciousness, one of the most visible oriental missionary advances in recent years.

For American Christians this is a strange turn of events. Since the English cobbler-turned-preacher William Carey sailed to India almost two centuries ago, western missionaries have been going to the Orient carrying the Gospel to Hindus, Buddhists, and followers of other pagan religions. But in recent years the missionary traffic has become two-way, with hundreds of eastern gurus, yogas, babas, and swamis coming to find a ripe mission field here.

The *Spiritual Community Guide for North America* (Spiritual Community Publishers, San Rafael, California) lists hundreds of societies, orders, foundations, centers for spiritual awareness, and self-realization groups. Most are rooted in the pantheistic religions of the East. Many are only small, local, meditative, reflective communities seeking a higher consciousness and union with the cosmic Mind of the universe. Some, such as Hare Krishna and the Divine Light Mission (see next chapter), are aggressively branching out to establish centers in every sizable city.

Let us first take a capsuled look at Hinduism, because it is the mother religion of the Hare Krishna movement.

Hinduism is often acclaimed as the oldest religion in the world. Hardly. The core Hinduistic doctrine of the cosmic oneness of God, man, and the universe was brought to North India around 2,000 B.C. by Aryan colonizers from Persia and Afghanistan who spoke Sanskrit, a linguistic ancestor of English.

The Aryans drew their basic belief from ancient Shinar, where men sought to build a tower "whose top may reach unto heaven" (Gen. 11:4). The name *Babylon* is derived from the Shinar tower, Babel, meaning "gate of God."

The Babylonians and Persians continued building ziggurats or cosmic mountains, in attempts to bring together heaven and earth. Priests, ascending to the astral altar at the top, acted out the stages of man's rise toward realization of oneness with the divine cosmos.

The monarch occupied the highest position and was worshiped as a god-man who kept society in harmony with the cosmic order. His occultish (hidden) knowledge was sought by the people in mystical rites of worship.

The forest gurus (spiritual teachers) of India had long been searching for higher knowledge. These men adopted the ideas of the arriving Aryans into their primitive belief system. The syncretism was passed along through oral tradition and incorporated into written form as the Vedas (sacred lore). The resulting religion eventually became known as Hinduism.

In Hinduism all is God and God is all. In the divine allness there is a whole pantheon of gods who incarnate themselves in living things from time to time. The three chief gods form a sort of Trinity: Brahma, the Creator; Vishnu, the Preserver; and Shiva, the Destroyer.

From Brahma came myriads of souls (*jivas*). Starting in the simplest forms of life, they have been transmigrating and reincarnating in higher forms through natural processes of death and birth. They will continue this flow until all have been fully absorbed into the Divine Essence.

In Hinduism, God is never wholly Other as the Bible teaches. Man is not separated from God by sin, but is already within the godhead. God is not reaching down to men in redemptive love, but man is climbing to self-realization through progressively higher levels of consciousness.

To understand man's ascent, as Hinduism defines it in various ways, certain key terms must be defined.

Karma is the cosmic law of cause and effect by which a soul transmigrates from one body to another. In karma all thoughts, motives, and actions affect the next reincarnation. Thus, one can blame every unfortunate situation in life on the misbehavior of a previous existence.

Maya is the way man views the world on his lowest level of consciousness. In maya the world is seen as separate things, not as one ultimate Essence. When viewed thus, the world appears full of sorrow, suffering, and confusion. But as man rises to higher levels of consciousness, viewing the world as oneness, placing himself at the center and not at the periphery of life, he becomes free from bondage to maya. At the top of the ascent, he comes into reality, that ultimate self-realization when nothing is seen as apart, when there is neither "I" nor "it," but only blissful oneness. Then man will have broken all links to the maya world of suffering and disorder, and will have become fully realized in the godhead.

Yogas are teachings which show how to reach this objective. *Yoga* has the same root as "yoke" and means to join or unite. *Yogis* are teachers who disseminate their yogas.

Hinduism has a whole cafeteria of yogas from which seekers may choose. They are like roads which ultimately arrive at the same destination, though some are more crooked and difficult than others. Thus a Hindu can say to a Christian or anyone else, "Your yoga is good, but mine is better."

Much Hindu terminology appears to parallel the teachings of Jesus. For example, the Raja Yoga speaks of five restraints (noninjury, truthfulness, nontheft, spiritual conduct, nongreed) and five observances (purity, serenity, austerity, study, attentiveness to God). However, Hindu and Christian theologies are quite different.

Hinduism says all roads ultimately lead to God.

Jesus said, "I am the Way, the Truth, and the Life: no man cometh to the Father, but by Me (John 14:6).

Hinduism says man is innately good, is within the Divine Essence, and can raise himself to the highest Reality.

Christianity says that, though man was created in the image of God, he has fallen away by disobedience and must be redeemed and made a new creation by the saving, atoning work of God in Christ.

Hinduism denies the real world of conflict and suffering, absolves individuals of responsibility for difficult situations, and urges retreat into self-consciousness instead of moving out to heal the hurts of humanity.

Christianity is active, not passive. One need only look at the healing institutions in India to see that most were started, staffed, and financed by Christian missions.

One of the Hindu gurus who came to America during the '60s was the aging Swami A. C. Bhaktivedanta Prabhupada. He claimed to be in a succession of disciples entrusted with the yoga of Lord Krishna, the eighth incarnation of Vishnu, the Preserver.

The god Krishna, whom Swami Prabhupada

claimed to represent, was quite a legendary hero. He is said to have had 16,000 wives and to have directed a battle in which 640 million Indians were killed.

Krishna emphasized detachment from materialism and discipline of mind to obtain peace. One "who keeps the senses under control and free from attachment and aversion, attains purity of spirit," he declared.

The key to a disciplined mind is devotion and surrender to Krishna. This surrender means giving up direction of one's life, and allowing life to flow unimpeded in sacramental worship to God.

Swami Prabhupada said he had been instructed by his own spiritual master to come to America. At 70 he left his considerable property behind and booked passage on a merchant ship. He carried only seven dollars, a suitcase of Vedic scriptures he had translated, and a letter of introduction to an Indian family.

He arrived in New York in 1965 unheralded. He went about as he had in India, speaking to restless, questing youth. His first disciples on the Lower East Side were mostly dropouts from straight society who had tried the drug and sex trips and were now looking for something else.

They rented a storefront and began street promotion of nightly meetings. Their first flyers declared: STAY HIGH FOREVER. NO COMING DOWN. PRACTICE KRISHNA-CONSCIOUSNESS . . . TURN ON THROUGH MUSIC, DANCE, PHILOSOPHY, SCIENCE, RELIGION, AND PRASDAM [spiritual food].

Scores of youth looking for a better trip jammed into the storefront. Prabhupada served them vegetarian meals and led in chanting the Krishna mantra, "Hare Krishna, Hare Krishna, Krishna, Krishna, Hare, Hare, Hare Rama, Hare Rama, Rama, Hare, Hare." It meant, he explained, "O Lord Krishna, O energy of Krishna, kindly engage me in Your service."

The swami challenged his followers to relinquish all material possessions and ambitions, cease illicit sexual activity and drug use, and devote themselves to Krishna's service. Despite the strange rituals and the odd dress adopted by devotees, the movement spread rapidly among counterculture youth in big cities. Beatle George Harrison became a devotee and his Krishna song, "My Sweet Lord," leaped to the top of the charts.

By 1976 there were 27 ashrams (communes) in the U.S. housing 3,000 robed and saried full-time workers, other communes in major European cities, a farm in West Virginia, a school for Krishna children in Dallas, a publishing house, an incense business, and a network of social service centers. And every Sunday thousands more were coming to join in ritual feasts at their local Krishna ashram.

The fervent Hare Krishnas appear to be the most intolerant of the Hindu sects in the West. Swami Prabhupada has said, "Anyone who does not know about Krishna is . . . either sinful, a rascal, the lowest of mankind, or his knowledge has been taken away by illusion."

There is no sacred-secular dichotomy with the militant Krishnas. Every act of life, from breathing to eating, is attuned to liberating the soul from the body and increasing Krishna-consciousness.

Take the chanting of the *mantra,* "Hare Krishna." Hindus have long recognized that sound vibrations affect the emotions. Just as music can alter moods and the monotony of rain falling on a roof can induce sleep, so the mantra can induce a trancelike ecstasy of spirit. It is said that the founder of the Krishna sect of Chaitanya chanted "Hare" in such rapture that he danced into the sea and drowned.

It is therefore a missionary work to persuade people to chant the mantra. This is why a Krishna solicitor will ask a passerby who declines to give a donation to at least say, "Hare Krishna." The devotee believes that Krishna-consciousness is present within everyone, and saying the mantra will help to awaken that consciousness.

Even the dress and appearance of the Krishna believer has deep meaning. The shaved head is a sign of detachment from pleasure. The white clay lines on the forehead suggest that the body is the temple of the cosmic God and must be used in his service. The male's pigtail is to make it easier for Lord Krishna to pull him into greater consciousness.

Life in a Krishna ashram is rigorous and hard by western standards. After rising to bathe at 3:30 A.M., devotees meditate and chant until breakfast, about 7:45. After that come classes and housework until 9:15, when the regular workday begins. Members are assigned various tasks by their local president. One may package incense while another designs art layouts for the next issue of the *Back to Godhead* magazine. Others may go into the streets to sell literature and evangelize. Not until 10 P.M. are they allowed to fall into exhausted sleep. The thought behind every task is to arouse more Krishna consciousness within oneself and the world.

Lord Krishna's legendary 16,000 wives notwithstanding, modern devotees strive for purity and to be free from passion. Any dress, situation, book, movie, or conversation that might stir sexual desire must be avoided. Marriages are arranged and approved by high-ranking members. Husbands and wives may not kiss or pet and may have intercourse only once a month—at the best time for procreation. Before coming together, they chant several hours to cleanse their minds.

Swami Prabhupada claims "no distinction is made on the basis of sex," that Krishna-consciousness is "given to both men and women equally." But he thinks the Indian practice in which a woman is under the care and responsibility of her husband is best. This keeps a man from impregnating a woman and leaving her to fend for herself.

However, women appear to occupy lower positions in the organization and to be regarded as inferiors to men. This may be why men reportedly outnumber women three to one in the Hare Krishna movement.

While the first wave of Hare Krishnas came largely from the drug culture, the cult has been more successful in winning other types in recent years. A recent issue of *Back to Godhead* ran interviews with a chemist and a mathematician. Both held earned doctorates when they joined the group.

The chemist, who once worked for the National Bureau of Standards, recalled being struck by Swami Prabhupada's statement that "everything could be understood in terms of a personal basis, rather than on an impersonal basis." "I began to understand," he wrote, "that personalism was superior to impersonalism. . . . [Swami] Prabhupada's concept was more all-encompassing, consistent, and rational. So I accepted it."

His math colleague noted that he had pursued science for many years "to find out what the absolute truth is . . . but by graduate school I had come to the conclusion that mathematics was not leading me to the truth, but to the void." He realized "there had to be something beyond mathematics, which didn't make sense according to my scientific training. . . . Then I came to Krishna-consciousness. It was what I'd been looking for."

Krishna devotees revere Swami Prabhupada. They are not likely to admit he has ever been wrong. But in an interview with the *Los Angeles Times* in 1968, Prabhupada insisted that the forthcoming manned landings on the moon would not occur, or if astronauts did land, they would be opposed by nearly invisible creatures of higher intelligence. He cited Hindu Vedic writings as the source for this knowledge. He also said that according to Vedic literature the moon is farther from earth than the sun.

The swami's followers have recently run into difficulty soliciting donations. They claim they were driven out of Winnipeg, Canada by the local Civic Charities Endorsement Bureau, the agency that issues fund-raising permits. At the San Francisco International Airport they, along with other cultists, are liable to arrest if caught begging. At Chicago's O'Hare Airport they are tolerated but watched closely.

Two clashes between Christian youth passing out literature and Hare Krishnas have been reported in newspapers.

In Montreal a Christian girl working with a literature team at the 1976 Olympics offered a tract to a Krishna girl, saying, "I love you and Jesus loves you." The cultist reacted angrily and slapped the Christian.

As the Christian turned to leave, another Hare Krishna shouted, "You insulted my sister," and slapped her so hard she fell to the ground. A hippie type, looking on, remarked to the Krishna solicitor, "You people talk about love, but I've just seen today where the real love is."

A month later in the Los Angeles Airport, a Hare Krishna allegedly told a young Jews for Jesus evangelist, "Get out of here, you're hurting my book sales."

"Are you threatening me?" the Hebrew Christian asked.

"You bet I'm threatening you," the Krishna devotee replied and brought a heavy hard cover book down on the Jew's head.

The cultist was arrested on charges of assault. The fiercest opposition to the Hare Krishna movement comes from parents who have lost children to the organization. Many have made charges similar to those leveled against Moon's Unification Church: brainwashing, isolation and alienation from family, regimentation into virtual slavery, and in some instances shipment out of the country under assumed names.

The following testimony, filed for the Day of Affirmation and Protest in Washington, D.C., is illustrative of parental complaints:

He had always been a very good student, good athlete, and always had several close friends. . . . We were extremely proud of him. He was loving and devoted to us—his parents, as well as his grandparents, aunts, uncles, and cousins. . . .

The radical change in our son's behavior and

personality since he joined this group is hard to believe; he is a totally different person—dehumanized and zombielike. He has abandoned his entire past life; has no interest in former friends, nor in any of his family. His calls and letters are very few and far between, despite our numerous attempts to communicate with him. When we do speak with him it can never be on a personal level; it is strictly a sermonizing type of conversation. There have been serious illnesses within our immediate family, but his responses have been negative, completely devoid of emotion.

The Hare Krishnas, like the Moonies, say parents simply do not understand the aspirations of their children. In deference to the group in Toronto, the *Toronto Star* permitted Ms. Bivhavati Dasi (alias Eve Norton) to tell her story in the paper. Some excerpts:

After graduating from McGill (University) in 1975 with an honors degree in history, I had become aware that the '60s were a time of religious, political, and moral crisis. The burden of resolution, it seemed to me, rested on the shoulders of the youth.

When the flower children wilted and Timothy Leary turned into a drunk, I realized that drugs were not going to help.

Ms. Dasi recalled seeing Krishnas on the street and deciding to visit the Krishna temple in Toronto. It was another dimension in human behavior. Under the pretext of writing a newspaper article, I . . . interviewed the devotees there.

Soon afterwards I traded in my pants for a

sari and replaced my cigarette with a string of prayer beads. I became one of the Hare Krishna people. . . .

Our message, as we stand chanting on the street corners of all the big cities in the world, is that it is not so important to change what you do, but that you must change what you are.

Opposition to the Krishna challenge appears to be intensifying. But the movement is not likely to dissipate soon. The defection rate is estimated to be only about 30 per cent the first year and about 10 per cent thereafter. The cult is winning more than enough new followers to fill the gaps.

Concerned, thoughtful persons must view the Krishna adherents from two perspectives:

One, of pity, because they have apparently turned their wills over to a swami who teaches a religion of retreat from the opportunity to develop as free persons and to dedicate their youthful vigor to more constructive causes.

Two, of admiration, because of their unwavering devotion to their beliefs in ways that put nominal Christians to shame.

As Pat Boone says:

When the Krishnas stop me in an airport, I tell them what Christ has done for me. When they ask me to say, "Hare Krishna," my response is, "No, but I'll say, 'Jesus is Lord.' "

I really admire the way they give their whole life to their cause. But I wish they could see as I have seen the degradation and suffering in eastern countries where Hinduism is so prevalent.

4

"Divine Light" From a Teenage Deity?

The much-indulged Maharaj Ji is not your typical Satguru (Perfect Living Master). He likes night-clubbing, drinking, dancing, and racing about in fast sports cars. Portly and sometimes petulant, he has been known to react like the teenager he is.

Reporter: "Are you the son of God?"

Maharaj Ji: "Everybody's the son of God. You ain't the uncle or aunt of God, are you?"

This round-faced, dark-eyed Satguru is the most revered teenager in the world. To some six million believers (mostly in India; 60,000 in the U.S.), he is a god-man, ranking with Jesus of Nazareth and Gautama Buddha.

Like Father Moon and Swami Prabhupada, this Perfect Master is a guru-come-lately on the American scene. Also like them, he has had astonishing success. He has also had troubles, which we will describe later.

Young Maharaj Ji was born into Hindu divinity on December 10, 1957. His father, Shri Hans Ji, then regarded as the current Perfect Living Master, headed the worldwide Divine Light Mission (DLM). Maharaj Ji was the youngest of three sons, but his ailing father announced he would be the next incarnation of the Master.

After his father's death in 1966, the boy took over leadership of the DLM's far-flung operation: 480 ashrams in 38 countries, a film company, a recording studio, a publishing house, an airline, a travel agency, an electronics firm, a theater chain, and even a janitorial service. As Perfect Master he was entitled to a 60 per cent rake-off on the profits.

In 1971, Maharaj Ji, only 14 and still living in India, lucked on to a publicity rocket that propelled him into the media limelight in the United States. It happened this way.

Rennie Davis, a leader in the antiwar student movement, was flying to Paris for talks with the Communist Vietcong. On the same plane was a film crew bound for India to shoot some footage of the Perfect Living Master. Davis was skeptical about their claims of the powers of the teenage Satguru, but he accepted their challenge to go and see for himself.

Davis met the youth and was profoundly impressed. Returning home, he told an incredulous student audience, "I've felt . . . the incredible joy which can await us all. Maharaj Ji is putting together a movement to end war, poverty, and hunger."

When the young Master came to America to capitalize on the publicity, Davis declared, "The Creator has come to help us pull the world back together again."

Other antiwar leaders felt no joy. Angry at Davis

for what seemed to be a betrayal of their cause, they threw cherry pies and tomatoes when he spoke in Berkeley. In a debate with Davis, Paul Krassner, editor of *The Realist,* compared the arrival of Maharaj Ji to the "second coming of Santa Claus." And clownish Abbie Hoffman, one of Davis' codefendants at the trial of the "Chicago Seven," muttered bitterly that if the Satguru was really an incarnation of God, then he was "what the United States of America deserved."

The publicity turned Maharaj Ji into a national celebrity and drew thousands of young seekers to DLM ashrams.

They were told that the DLM was not a separate religion, that Maharaj Ji respected all holy books, though he quoted most from the Hindu scriptures because they were oldest. Mahatmas (holy men) advised them not to attempt to analyze the DLM, because thinking could be a hindrance, and cited Maharaj Ji as saying that questioning "creates terrible suffering in your mind." Instead, seekers should look to the Perfect Master for divine knowledge.

Thousands took the challenge and begged to receive the "knowledge." What the "premies" (beginners) experienced is described by a defector:

About 12 or 15 of us were led into a dark room where we faced a mahatma spotlighted against a wall. He warned us about the ill fortune any would suffer who dared to reveal the secrets of the ceremony. Then he began the ritual.

First, he pressed his knuckles hard against my eyeballs and held them there until I saw the Divine Light. Next, he jammed his fingers into my ears in a peculiar way until I heard music, the Divine Harmony. Then he shoved me back into the meditative position and I tasted the Divine Nectar—mucus! Finally he gave me a secret word to meditate on, a funny kind of sound that was supposed to signify divine energy. That's all. I was in.

Initiated premies moved into communal ashrams where they lived a tightly structured, celibate life, spending hours in meditation, subsisting on a vegetarian diet, and doing any service requested by their leaders. Always, they were taught to purge the mind of all doubts by meditating thoughts into blackness. And always they were to accept without question any instruction on the spiritual life from the Perfect Master, issued through a mahatma.

As youths continued joining, DLM leaders were cagey and cautious about what was said in public *satsang* (spiritual community meetings). An effort was made to use Christian terminology, which often came out ludicrous. For example, Mahatma Rajeshwar is credited with saying, "You see, Christ was not crucified for forgiving sins of human beings. Sin is forgiven by meditation. Because where is the sin? Sin is in the mind."

Deifying statements were made about Maharaj Ji. Mahatma Rajeshwar declared, "Perfect Master is no human being. He is living God on this earth." Another mahatma said he was the fulfillment of biblical prophecies of the second coming of Christ. And the Maharaj himself said without reservation, "I will rule the world, and just watch how I will do it."

By 1972 the young Master was reported to be living quite well, dividing his time between a

$400,000 estate in Malibu, California and an $80,000 pad in Denver; and traveling to satsang in a $50,000 Rolls Royce equipped with a refrigerator and other conveniences. All fruits of tax-exempt businesses and free labor by his followers.

His mahatmas were whooping up Millenium '73 when the Perfect Master would usher in the Perfect Age. The "most significant event in the history of humanity" was to be held in Houston's Astrodome, November 8. The cosmic timing seemed perfect. On November 7 the moon and the planets Venus, Pluto, and Saturn would be at right angles, forming the Grand Cross. The next day the constellation Aquarius would rise in the west, symbolizing to the astrological world the dawning of the Age of Aquarius.

Also at that time the Comet Kohoutek would be nearing the earth. Prophets and seers were predicting the direst tragedies to accompany the comet's arrival.

As Millenium '73 approached, the Maharaj's devotees became more and more excited. One story circulated that a UFO would land. Accordingly, spaces were left in the Astrodome parking lot for the extraterrestrial ship. Another story moved among the ashrams that the Astrodome and the worshipful crowd would ascend to heaven.

The DLM rented the Astrodome for three days at $25,000 a day. The Maharaj and his "holy family," mother and brothers, were ensconced in the Celestial Suite of the Astroworld Hotel which tycoons ordinarily took for $2,500 a day.

Only a third of an expected 60,000 people showed up. Still the DLM put on quite a show. Bhole Ji, one of the Maharaj's brothers, directed the rock band Blue Aquarius in an ear-shattering rendition of "O Lord of the Universe." Then the Perfect Master addressed his subjects from a blue velvet throne high above the Astrodome floor while his round-faced image flashed in lights on the stadium scoreboard.

When the celebration ended it was evident no significant event had occurred. The parking spaces reserved for the UFOs were still empty. The disappointed followers had to clear out quickly and make way for the next day's pro football game.

More jolts for the DLM faithful were yet to come. In May 1974, Maharaj Ji took out a marriage license to marry his 24-year-old secretary, Marilyn Johnson. Being underage he had to get permission from a Colorado judge. The judge consented, noting that the teenage lord appeared quite mature and could afford a bride.

Marilyn was a non-Hindu, former airline stewardess. No matter. Her husband, the Perfect Master, had the perfect idea. He promptly proclaimed her the incarnation of the ten-armed, tiger-taming goddess Durga.

Next, news broke that tax investigators were peeking at the DLM's account books. The Mission was over $200,000 in debt, and expenses for the "most significant event in history" had been paid under considerable pressure.

As if this were not enough, the Maharaj's "Revered Mother," Mataji, deposed her lordly son for "living a nonspiritual way of life" and declared his brother Sat Pal would lead the DLM empire in his place. She explained that her late husband had intended for the elder brother to be the Perfect Master before Maharaj Ji was born. It was she who had installed the younger Maharaj Ji as the Perfect Master. Now she realized this had been a mistake.

What had prompted the shakeup in the "holy family"? Outsiders speculated that Maharaj Ji and his bride had been disrespectful of the Revered Mother during her visit to the United States. Reportedly, the newlyweds had banned her from their Malibu mansion and had replaced her pictures in ashrams with photos of themselves.

Maharaj Ji refused to step down. He filed suit in India against his elder brother. The brother sued back. After the squabble was aired in Indian newspapers, the contending brothers promised a New Delhi judge they would try to settle out of court. "Well, there is going to be bloodshed in your family unless you do" the judge warned. Followers of the teenage "god" were confused. Some were reportedly so shattered they committed suicide.

The dispute continued over who was the rightful Perfect Master, while Maharaj Ji returned to the United States with his wife to resume control of the American operation.

Since the lordly flap, more trouble has erupted for the young claimant to deity.

In Canada a suit came before the British Columbia Supreme Court seeking to prevent heiress Darby McNeal from signing over an estimated $400,000 inheritance to the DLM. Canadian theologian Dr. Joseph I. Richardson testified for the plaintiffs that Maharaj Ji "apparently does not have a life-style which in any way corresponds to the ideals of traditional Indian gurus." The DLM, Dr. Richardson said, is "one of the many contemporary eclectic religious movements which depends for its existence and growth on the exploitation of the confusion and disillusionment of largely middle-class young people . . . disaffected with society in general."

And in Washington, D.C. the Minnesota mother of a DLM member presented a damaging testimony on the Day of Affirmation and Protest.

The mother related how her daughter, Kerstin, "an above-average student," became involved in the Mission while on a Rotary Club exchange program in India. When she returned home, the mother said, she stared at the picture of the pudgy Maharaj Ji and sometimes went into a "strange trance" for hours.

When Maharaj Ji set up headquarters in Denver, the daughter moved to an ashram there. She gave much of her savings and solicited a gift from her aged aunt for the Mission, while she herself worked and begged, getting only three and four hours of sleep a night.

After DLM leaders sent her to Germany, her father flew there and tried to talk with her. But he was permitted to see her only in the presence of another DLM member.

Kerstin was still in the DLM, the mother said sadly. Two of her girl friends who had left the Mission had committed suicide.

More negative testimonies were circulated by parents' groups already active against the Unification Church, Hare Krishna, and other cults. Bill West, for example, recalled for the Citizens' Freedom Foundation his experience with the DLM:

The persuasion (that life should be perfect) started in one of my required education courses at Michigan State University. We . . . [were] led to believe that we could be happier, healthier, and better educated for living through such learning techniques as meditation and biofeedback. The popular literature . . . being sold near the campus . . . added to this picture through such titles as *Be Here Now*, by Dr. Richard Alpert (alias Bada Ram Das), and Carlos Castenada's books about Yaqui Indian sorcery. These books had a countercultural bias, and presented the idea of a spiritual teacher who enriches his followers' lives by imparting arcane spiritual knowledge.

Several of my friends had studied Maharishi Yogi's Transcendental Meditation . . . I had just started to save my $75 initiation fee, however, when I received an interesting newsletter from a devotee of another guru. . . .

Encouraged, I attended a public meeting on the MSU campus the next week. I was fascinated by what I saw there. Short-haired, clean-shaven young men in business suits and pretty young women in immaculate granny dresses were singing devotional songs. All seemed to be serene, ecstatic, or incredibly loving. Entranced, I sought out the young man who had written the newsletter.

The point at which, and the degree to which, I lost my free will in my original encounters with the guru's devotees is difficult to determine because a variety of techniques were being used to ensnare the converts. Marc, the author of the newsletter, had a peculiar persuasive ability. At our first encounter, I perceived that he was both totally sane and the first person I had ever met who had been completely open and honest with me. Within one month, I was convinced that whatever he told me came directly from God, and that I had no choice but to obey him. He directed me to go follow Mahatma Parlokanand from city to city until I had received the Knowledge, and I left that day. . . .

That the mahatma was a hypnotist . . . did not enter my mind at the time. The mahatma was presented as a saint, and a *realized* disciple of the guru. After 8, 10, and sometimes 12 hours of daily indoctrination over a period of a week, I was admitted to a Knowledge Session. There under the guise of receiving the baptism of the Holy Spirit, I was hypnotized without my knowledge or consent. I wondered how I had lived for 25 years in the belief that I breathed through my nose when it was obvious that I was breathing through the top of my head.

Having been initiated . . . I was now ripe for further manipulation. The hypnotic high was reinforced by meditation. . . . Every time I had an independent thought, I felt uneasy and sat and concentrated on my breath until my mind stopped thinking. At this point, I would accept almost anything my leaders told me, since I was not capable of questioning anything.

I was asked one day whether I would die for the Guru Maharaj Ji, and when I replied that I would, I was told that I was making progress quickly. In fact, if the Guru had instructed me to murder my mother at that time, I would have done so without hesitation, confident that I was doing her a favor. It was about this time that I began to lose my possessions. Some things I gave to the guru of my own free will, because the other devotees made me feel guilty if I didn't, but other things were taken away and sold without my consent.

I spent nine months in this state, meditating constantly, seeking new converts, and trying to get more money for the guru. Finally, when I was at home, recovering from an accident . . . my mother introduced a deprogrammer, Ted Patrick, who sat and questioned me for two hours. At the end of that time I was thinking again.

Paul Myette, an ex-DLM devotee from Boston, left the organization via another route. In a "Dear Premies" letter published by the Spiritual Counterfeits Project of Berkeley, Myette recounted what happened to him.

"I was really excited by the blowout satsang given to me by some friends who were experiencing the meditation. It took no time at all to realize that all the premies I saw were very, very high and that I wanted to receive this knowledge."

Paul went chasing after a mahatma. "I was so empty and hungry . . . that when Mahatma Ji revealed the 'light' to me, it was so intense that my head flew back. It was like being hit by a train—and I dug it."

He became a fervent worshiper of Maharaj Ji and an active evangelist for the DLM in Boston. One summer day he was "out propagating" for a local program at which the guru was scheduled to speak. He greeted a man on the street, handed him a leaflet, and started telling about The Knowledge and how Maharaj Ji was on earth to "manifest Christ to man."

He told me that he was a Christian and that he

was experiencing the love of God through His only begotten Son, the man, Christ Jesus. I told him that his faith was a good thing, but that he could directly experience God through the Knowledge and "see the light." This man told me that he needed no link to God other than Jesus Christ and that Jesus expressly warned against false christs.

This man was practically glowing in the dark as he lovingly spoke to me. He told me to investigate Jesus and open my heart to Him. He said that if I prayed to Him and asked Him to enter my heart, He would touch my soul and fill me with love.

I began to perform an experiment. For three days I didn't meditate. I felt very empty. I was reading the Bible over these three days, and I was realizing the uniqueness of Jesus. It came to a point that I was so torn that I said, "OK, Jesus, I know You are Lord. Touch my heart, Lord, fill me with Your life. Let me know right now if Your Spirit is that same spirit that's in Guru Maharaj Ji." At that point, I felt a love so strong in my heart . . . that it forced tears out of my eyes—a totally different, deeper, more beautiful love than Guru Maharaj Ji's. I understood that Jesus was touching me and filling me. I realized that I had called and He had really answered.

"Please check it out for yourself," Paul begged his premie friends, "and you'll find that Jesus is the only way to the Lord. I've been where you are. I've experienced the Knowledge *intensely* and I've experienced God through Jesus Christ. They are not the same. Jesus is the only way to the Father."

Besides losing hundreds of members such as Paul Myette and Bill West, the DLM has suffered serious financial reverses because of the "holy family's" feud and other disillusioning situations. In 1976 American donations dropped from more than $100,000 a month to $30,000. The printing business along with some other property has been sold. The lease on the computer that once kept track of Guru Maharaj Ji's followers has been dropped.

The teenage guru's divinity is not emphasized so much. Joe Anctil, the 43-year-old spokesman for the DLM, simply describes him as "the point of inspiration for all of us."

However, members still revere their guru, despite his extravagant life-style. His pictures hang on every wall of their three-story international headquarters in Denver. A newspaper, *Divine Times,* and a magazine, *And It Is Divine,* are still published.

The mission still predicts that their perfect Master will bring in an era of perfect peace. They talk of building their own Divine City where the Master will himself rule over his flock.

The Divine Light Mission may be flickering but it is far from fading away.

5

TM: Religion
or Relaxer?

A quick way to start a heated argument in many groups is to ask, "What do you think about TM*?"

Before you can say "TM" three times, opinions may be falling like hail:

"TM proves P. T. Barnum was right. 'A sucker is born every minute.'"

"TM is the best thing since penicillin. It relaxes tense muscles, tranquilizes the mind, restores energy, increases alpha brain-wave production, improves memory, lowers blood pressure. . . ."

"You've been brainwashed. TM is a subversive, deceptive way of passing Hinduism into western society."

Faith or fraud, therapy or threat, Maharishi Mahesh Yogi's Transcendental Meditation is now the daily practice of 600,000 Americans from the halls of ivy to the sweatshops of industry. Senator Ted Kennedy, Mary Tyler Moore, and many other

---

* TM is a registered trademark.

prominent personalities are said to practice TM. The Maharishi anticipates that by 1980, 40 million people will be repeating a sacred mantra for two 20-minute periods each day, and that they will change the world.

The TM phenomenon is even being promoted by governmental bodies and officials. Consider:

—The Illinois State House of Representatives passed a resolution asking "that all educational institutions, especially those under state jurisdiction, be strongly encouraged to study the feasibility of courses in Transcendental Meditation and the Science of Creative Intelligence (a division of the TM conglomerate)." This after a legislator testified Transcendental Meditation had saved his two children from drugs.

—The Honorable Thomas P. Salmon, Governor of Vermont, issued a proclamation praising TM for removing "the main cause of hypertension, anxiety, high blood pressure, and other psychosomatic illnesses"; offering a solution to drug abuse, and promoting "improvement in student behavior, and in student-parent and teacher relationships." He declared the week following, "World Plan Week," in respect to the Maharishi's objectives, and urged all state employees to attend a special TM presentation.

—The National Institute of Health provided funds to train 130 high school instructors in TM's Science of Creative Intelligence at Humboldt State College, California.

Court suits have been filed contending that the practice of TM in public schools violates the separation of church and state. The central question at issue is whether TM is the expression of a religion or simply a technique for personal improvement, based on scientifically verified principles.

Let us look at some of the evidence the courts will undoubtedly be examining—the origin, introduction, promotion, and practice of Transcendental Meditation.

Historically, the form followed by TM is not unique or new. Mystic-minded Jews of the second century B.C. repeated the name of a magic seal. Islamic Sufists of the ninth century developed *zikr,* the repetition of a devout incantation of one of the "beautiful names of God." The practice was believed to lift the heart toward the highest self till the perfection of oneness with God was attained.

Repetitive prayers such as the Rosary have long been practiced by devout Roman Catholics. In the 14th century the anonymous author of the devotional classic *The Cloud of Unknowing* wrote that union with God requires a descent to lower levels of consciousness by eliminating all distractions and activity. God can be contacted directly, he said, by entering a "cloud of unknowing." Repeating a one-syllable word such as "God" or "love" is an aid in this process, he advised.

Modern Transcendental Meditation was brought to the West from India only about 20 years ago by Maharishi Mahesh Yogi, who still heads the worldwide meditative empire.

He was born Mahesh Brasad Warma into a middle-class Indian family in either 1911 or 1918 and educated as a physicist. Instead of following his vocation, he began a spiritual quest under the direction of a bearded Hindu religious leader known as Guru Dev. Before Dev died, he commissioned Mahesh to find a simple form of meditation that would be helpful to all classes of people, not just recluses and monks.

For two years Mahesh brooded and meditated in a cave in the Himalayas. Finally in the late '50s he emerged with the formula he called Trancendental Meditation and with a new title for himself, "Maharishi" (great sage).

The Maharishi tried to introduce TM in Madras, India's third largest city, but was lost in a sea of swamis, each claiming a secret way of knowing the Divine Mind better. In 1959 he headed for London, believing his new insight would have more chance of acceptance in the West. The English did not beat a path to his door, however, and for the next eight years he remained relatively unknown. Then he was discovered by the Beatles and suddenly the bearded hermit from the Himalayas became a worldwide figure.

Beatle George Harrison got acquainted with the Maharishi while studying Indian music. His enthusiasm spread to his colleagues and off they flew to a remote spot in Wales to study Transcendental Meditation with the Indian teacher. The story that the Beatles had turned to meditation made instant headlines around the world. "Transcendental Meditation is good for everyone," Paul McCartney was quoted as saying. "This is the biggest thing in our lives," was ascribed to John Lennon.

Shirley MacLaine, the Rolling Stones, Mia Farrow, and other show-business personalities jumped on the TM praise wagon. The Maharishi became the toast of the fast-living, psychedelic jet set. TV talk shows gobbled him up. His bearded picture in simple, white flowing robe, rubber-thonged sandals, and beads, graced major magazines. Universities grabbed at him as if he were the reincarnation of Francis of Assisi.

His message was always the same: meditating on a sacred word for two short periods every day would remove tension, melt hostility, and bring a nirvana of happiness.

Then the Beatles got bored and announced it was just another trip. A year after his discovery, the Maharishi was just another swami with a gimmick too simple to swallow.

The Maharishi flew back to India to recoup and reorganize. Within a couple of years he was back in the West. By 1972 *Time* was saying that the gentle guru had "generated what may well be the fastest growing cult in the West." And the TM bandwagon keeps rolling.

How has it happened? Is the Maharishi a merchandising genius? Or a spell-casting wizard?

Perhaps he is some of both, and a man ingenious enough to capitalize on the dissatisfaction felt by millions of Americans.

Following the departure of the Beatles and the publicity fadeout, the Maharishi began training a core of teachers. As they became proficient, he set them up as instructors in TM centers across the country. They trained others, who in turn opened more centers, until by 1976 the Maharishi was claiming over half a million active practitioners.

The best markets were on college campuses. As the practice caught on among faculty and students, two TM companies, the Student's International Meditation Society and the International Meditation Society, conducted "research" and released findings attesting to TM's benefits: helping break drug habits, increasing creativity, adding energy,

and so forth. One study at Harvard was ballyhooed
as showing that marijuana use dropped from 80 per
cent to 12 per cent among 1,862 TM practitioners
and use of LSD from 48 per cent to 3 per cent.

After a number of such claims appeared in press
releases, skeptics began conducting tests of their
own. One was University of Arizona psychologist
George Domino. He tested the creativity of four
groups of adults (35 members per group) over a
six-month period.

The first group practiced TM; the second par-
ticipated in a relaxation program that involved sitting comfortably in a quiet place and mentally
reciting a single-syllable sound of their choosing;
the third took a course in the psychology of creativity; the fourth pursued their regular life routine.

Only the 35 taking the psychology course showed
any significant increase in creativity.

TM publicists, of course, simply ignored such
negative research and kept pushing the favorable
claims in academic circles.

The first Science of Creative Intelligence training
course for academic credit was taught at Stanford
by the Maharishi's U.S. director. After that other
schools fell in line. By 1976 over 200 schools, including Yale and various branches of the University of
California, were said to allow credit for TM training courses.

Acceptance of TM on prestigious college campuses influenced high schools to get in the swing.
Credit courses in TM are now offered in high
schools from New York to California with federal
grants provided for training TM teachers. TM has
also been included in the U.S. Army's alcohol and
drug-abuse program.

But if the court suits are successful, TM classes will presumably be outlawed in public institutions and the federal fund spigot turned off.

In 1974 the Maharishi's managers purchased a 185-acre Iowa college campus with 72 buildings for the bargain-basement price of $2.5 million. Parsons College, operated for many years by Presbyterians and for a short time by an educational entrepreneur, was renamed Maharishi International University. TM publicists said it would be a prototype for other TM universities in the United States and abroad.

MIU now has about 500 students who look like the pride of Middle America. Boys wear suits and ties, girls wear skirts or dresses, and the only beard to be seen is on the picture of the Maharishi that hangs beside his old teacher, the Guru Dev, in prominent places.

A sampling of the core curriculum shows courses in astronomy; cosmology; physics and SCI (Science of Creative Intelligence)—Quantum Models of Pure Consciousness; Western Philosophy and SCI—From Plato's Republic to Maharishi's World Plan; and Vedic Philosophy and SCI—The Sources, Course, and Goal of Knowledge from Vedas to the Maharishi. Still MIU claims to be nonreligious. It has been accepted as a "candidate for accreditation" by the prestigious North Central Association of Colleges and Secondary Schools and is eligible for financial aid from the Department of Health, Education and Welfare.

Critics say that MIU's claim of being a non-religious university is deceptive as are some of the school's promotions. Regarding the latter, the March 28, 1975 issue of *Science* magazine (official journal of the American Association for the Advance of Science) reported Nobel Prize-winning chemist Melvin Calvin's charge that MIU's use of his name in the school's catalog came "perilously close to false advertising." Dr. Calvin, a faculty member of the University of California at Berkeley, said he had only spoken to a TM sponsored symposia. "He (the Maharishi) doesn't know anything about science," the Nobel laureate declared, "but does know that cloaking his dogma in scientific jargon is a way to gain legitimacy."

TM's acceptance has spread into many mainline Protestant churches which have opened their religious education facilities to classes. Some Protestant ministers testify that TM has transformed their lives. For instance, John Dilley, pastor of the First United Presbyterian Church in Fairfield, Iowa, the small town where Maharishi International University is located, claims that TM "clears" his mind for prayer and prepares his family for meaningful devotions together.

Most Protestant and Catholic churchmen and theologians differ. They say that by no stretch of the imagination can TM be compared with the meditation and reflection encouraged in Christian Scriptures.

When the psalmist declared, "I will meditate in Thy precepts" (119:15), he meant reflection on God's promises, laws, and ways. When he said, "I meditate on all Thy works; I muse on the work of Thy hands" (143:5), he certainly was not talking about repeating a hidden mantra word over and over.

To meditate, according to the definition of the Shorter Oxford Dictionary, is "to reflect upon, to study, ponder . . . to exercise the mind in thought or contemplation."

From a Christian perspective, meditation is, according to Gordon Chilvers, "taking a passage (of Scripture) or two and turning it over and over in our minds. This kind of reflection will establish the truth in our hearts and minds."

We return to the key question: Is TM a religious practice or not?

Few realize "the interior teaching of TM is avowedly Hindu," says Glenn Igleheart of the Southern Baptist Home Mission Board's Department of Interfaith Witness. "Any religious organization in America," he added in *Home Missions* magazine, "has the right to promulgate its teaching, but TM should acknowledge its Hindu origin and philosophy."

Billy Graham told the *National Enquirer* that TM practitioners

. . . don't know what they are letting themselves in for. . . . The danger doesn't lie so much in meditation itself as it does in what is chosen to meditate on. Meditation is like atomic energy, which can be used for the benefit of mankind, or for its destruction. . . . What goes into that empty space (in the mind) is the hidden danger of TM. It can be an invasion of satanic influences which will have an adverse effect on their lives.

Dr. Richard A. Mangin, editor of the *Catholic Voice* of the Oakland (Calif.) diocese, said bluntly, "What is absolutely crucial for Catholics to understand about Transcendental Meditation is that it is a form of Hinduism with tenets that conflict with basic Christian teaching and Christian religious experience. Properly understood and accepted, a person who embraces TM is changing religions."

The General Presbytery of the Assemblies of God adopted a resolution at its 1976 official meeting calling the practice of TM "a religious activity, not just an outlet for relaxation." The report said TM is contrary to the Bible doctrines of God, man, and salvation, and denies the existence of a personal God and the Creator-creature distinction. TM also "ignores the possible causes of psychological stress, offering only temporary relief."

Jack Wyrtzen, of the Word of Life Fellowship, calls TM "the power of positive nonthinking." He says the Maharishi has had "a devilish influence . . . on multitudes of people." In protesting the TM proclamation by the governor of Vermont, Wyrtzen asked Governor Salmon,

Are you not the least suspicious that out of poverty-stricken, disease-ridden India, with its continual problems, comes the claimed answer to all of life's problems? Would it not seem plausible that we could expect to see some evidence of accomplishment in the yogi's own land? . . . I have been to India. I have seen the harm these yogis have done to their country.

Governor Salmon replied to Wyrtzen:

There is as much religious connotation in the technique of TM as there is in a Dale Carnegie speaking course. What we have here is a technique, which can be of help to individuals who seek escape through drugs or alcohol when under stress. . . . It should not be confused with eastern mysticism. A religion it is not.

The Maharishi also claims that TM is not a religion, that, indeed, TM will make one a better practitioner of his own religion. But his claims seem contradictory. In *Meditations of the Maharishi Mahesh Yogi,* by Maharishi Mahesh Yogi, he says, "Transcendental Meditation is a path to God." And in replying to the question, "Is this meditation prayer?" the Maharishi replies, "[It is] a very good form of prayer which leads us to the field of the Creator, to the source of Creation, to the field of God" (Bantam Books, 1968, pp. 59, 95).

When the Maharishi first attempted to invade the West, he called his organization for spreading TM, the Spiritual Regeneration Movement. Later he stopped using the word "spiritual" and began emphasizing the "educational" and "scientific" benefits of TM. Did he recognize the latent suspicions of secular-minded westerners about religious gimmickry? Or did he realize that separation of church and state might be a legal barrier to TM in schools and other public institutions?

His statements in his book *The Science of Being and Art of Living* (Signet Books, 1968, pp. 298-300) provide an interesting comment:

Whenever and wherever religion dominates the mass consciousness, transcendental deep meditation should be taught in terms of religion. Whenever and wherever metaphysical thinking dominates the consciousness of society, transcendental deep meditation should be taught in metaphysical terms, openly aiming at the fulfillment of the current metaphysical thought. . . .

What is suited to the present generation? It seems, for the present, that this transcendental deep meditation should be made available to the peoples through the agencies of the government.

Putting aside the Maharishi's purported strategy, let us see if there is religious significance in the initiation ceremony.

The instruction fee of about $125 (students get a lower rate) pays for a personal interview and four daily two-hour sessions under an instructor approved by the Maharishi. Part of the time is devoted to the initiation ceremony.

You are asked to remove your shoes as you enter an incense-filled room lighted by flickering candles. You kneel before a fruit- and flower-covered altar featuring a color portrait of Guru Dev, the Maharishi's dead Hindu spiritual teacher.

Then your initiator bends over the altar and chants from memory an ancient Sanskrit hymn of adoration to Hindu deities and the departed masters of the Shankara tradition of Hinduism, while offering flowers, bits of rice, fruits, salt, and sandalwood before the portrait of Guru Dev. The hymn says in part,

To Lord Narayana, to lotus-born Brahma the Creator, to Vashishtha, to Shakti and his son Parashar,

. . . To Shankaracharya the redeemer, hailed as Krishna and Badarayana, to the commentator of the Brahma Sutras, I bow down.

To the glory of the Lord I bow down again and

again, at whose door the whole galaxy of gods pray for perfection day and night.

Adorned with immeasurable glory, preceptor of the whole world, having bowed down to him we gain fulfillment.

Skilled in dispelling the cloud of ignorance of the people, the gentle emancipator, Brahmananda Sarasvati, the supreme teacher, full of brilliance, him I bring to my awareness.

. . . Guru Dev, Shri Brahmananda, bliss of the Absolute, transcendental joy, the Self-Sufficient, the embodiment of pure knowledge which is beyond and above the universe like the sky, the aim of "Thou art That" and other such expressions which unfold eternal truth, the One, the Eternal, the Pure, the Immovable, the Witness of all intellects, whose status transcends thought, the Transcendent along with the three gunas, the true preceptor, to Shri Guru Dev, I bow down.

The blinding darkness of ignorance has been removed by applying the balm of knowledge. The eye of knowledge has been opened by him and therefore, to him, to Shri Guru Dev, I bow down.

While repeating the *puja* ritual, the instructor recites the words in Sanskrit and copies every movement prescribed for making the various offerings. You may not know what your initiator is chanting. But you are a participant by virtue of bringing fruit and flowers to be offered. Yet Jonathan Shear, professor of philosophy at MIU, insists that the initiatory rite to the practice of TM "is not a religious ceremony at all."

At the end of your initiation ceremony, you are assigned a *mantra,* a mystical word from Sanskrit, which you are to keep secret. As you repeat your mantra over and over for 15 to 20 minutes twice daily, the process will expand your conscious mind and bring it into contact with the creative intelligence behind every thought. Once you are in harmony with the universe, your inner conflicts will begin to slip away, contentment and bliss will permeate your being, and all your problems will disappear. When enough people are practicing TM, the world will become enveloped in sweetness and peace.

There is no regimentation, discipline, or mind control involved, your instructor assures you. You simply repeat and concentrate on your mantra, let your mind relax, and the kingdom of peace and tranquility will be yours to enjoy.

One of the plaintiffs in lawsuits filed against TM teaching and practice in public schools is the Spiritual Counterfeits Project, a ministry of the evangelical Berkeley Christian coalition. In preparation for its legal action, Spiritual Counterfeits Project has gathered testimonies from former TM practitioners and users. One such is Richard D. Scott, a former TM teacher who was involved with TM for six years. Scott has testified for the public record that while in training at Estes Park, Colorado, someone raised the question of TM being a religious teaching.

The question was prompted during one evening lecture, "Maharishi, why can't we teach TM in a religious garb?" The answer to that was, "This is a scientific age. Religion is not generally accepted. Therefore, if we talk in terms of religion"—mind you, this is a paraphrase—"it will not be accepted. Therefore, we have to speak in terms of the scientists. Maybe a day will come, perhaps in a couple of years, when we will be able to take off the robe of the scientist and put on the religious garb, talking in terms of God and devotion. But for now we must teach in scientific terms."

Scott further testified that as he advanced in TM, two more words were added to his secret mantra, making it *shri Aaing namah*.

So at this point in my own personal experience in meditation my mantra could be translated as oh, most beautiful Aaing (the name of a Hindu god), I bow down to you.

It seems hard to believe that promoters can deny the religiosity of TM. But in the context of Hinduism where all is God and God is all, this is quite understandable. There is no external God to which man must answer. The answer to man's problems is in himself. The key to solution, the Maharishi proclaims, is in Transcendental Meditation.

The Maharishi and his managers claim that TM is amenable to any religion. Within the world view of Hinduism this may be so. But from the perspective of orthodox Christianity, there can be no accommodation.

The Maharishi says "TM is a path of God." Christianity says Jesus is the Way, the Truth, and the Life. There is no other.

The Maharishi denies sin, evil, and personal responsibility, all of which Christianity affirms as reality.

The Maharishi teaches that man is himself divine and can reach "cosmic consciousness" through TM. If unattainable in this life, the soul can reach it in another existence. Christianity says that man is sinful and must be reconciled to God through the perfect Sacrifice, Jesus Christ.

The Maharishi teaches that suffering can be denied in oneself and one's fellowman. Christianity says that the disciples of Jesus may not retreat but must become healing ambassadors in the real world of pain and sin and frustration.

A California practitioner stopped meditation after three years because TM could not deliver "on the most important of all the promises it makes: the promise to produce a true solution to the human condition, the promise to produce a fundamental healing of the spiritual sickness of man." In his testimony, published by the Spiritual Counterfeits Project, he declared:

> The reason that TM cannot truly deal with the fact of death is that it cannot truly deal with the fact of our alienation from God, which is the source of death. Indeed the Maharishi teaches that there is only one reality in existence, which is God; that we are by nature a part of that Divine Reality, and only by ignorance or illusion do we falsely think ourselves cut off from it. The Maharishi's error is a common one. In meditation (TM) we transcend the forms of conceptual thought and experience the deep unity of our own being. Because Man is made in the image of God, it is easy to mistake this for an experience of God, or of union with God.

The "central problem" of TM, according to the Spiritual Counterfeits Project companion newspaper *Right On* (now published as *Radix*) is simply that TM

fails to introduce us to the One who is the source of morality. It names, instead, an abstract, extended version of ourselves as the origin of ourselves and of our conscience. Its flaw is not that it dispenses with morality, but that it puts moral judgment into our own hands by promising spontaneous right action to the one who meditates.

The human race doesn't need a technique for getting in touch with its inner essence. Humanity instead needs redemption, and that must come from without. We must agree with our Author to be "edited," and not yield to the temptation of a self-erasure that glorifies an empty page.

If TM then is so obviously non-Christian, even anti-Christian in the views of many, how can its appeal to the "Christian" West be explained? Another writer for the Spiritual Counterfeits Project thinks that

the growing popularity of groups like Transcendental Meditation in this country is symptomatic of the loss of the "Christian consensus" in America. We do live in a "post-Christian" world, a world so spiritually starved that occult philosophies and Eastern religions are finding fertile ground for their seas of delusion, deceit, and ultimate emptiness.

Theologian Krister Stendahl, dean of the Harvard Divinity School, agrees that spiritual starvation has opened the door to TM. "A genuine hunger for mystical experiences," he declares, "is the most significant fact about the TM craze."

Adds Ted Wise, a former leader in the Jesus People movement who has counseled a number of TMers and has studied Eastern religions and lived in the East, "I have found that Christians who have had a genuine encounter with Jesus Christ are not attracted to the TM movement. It is those who haven't who are hoping to find mystical experiences through it."

6

The Gurus
Keep Coming

Krishna Consciousness, the Divine Light Mission, and TM are only the most publicized manifestations of Hinduism in the West. Hundreds of other consciousness-raising spin-offs of Hinduism are alive in the West, each with its own guru claiming special powers of divinity.

Some are over a half century old and have recently taken a second wind. Some have sprung up during the past decade. Some may be dissolved by the time this book appears in print.

They share many traits of the stronger and more familiar eastern religious movements: man-centeredness, universal divinity, self-seeking and self-reliance, worship without ethical absolutes, and beliefs that may be irrational to traditional western thinking.

They are spreading faster than encroaching kudzu vines across the landscape of the West.

Let's survey a potpourri of the most noticeable movements.

The small sign over the door announcing the *Holy Order of Mans* and the cross on the wall suggest a Roman Catholic or Greek Orthodox retreat house. Much of the order's terminology adds to this impression. It speaks of "serving the sacraments," attending "seminary," taking "final vows," and "ordaining priests." The order also "worships" in "Sunday services." Its standard garb continues the camouflage, except that the long dark robe and clergy-collar worn with a large chromium cross dangling from a purple ribbon around the neck suggest a foreign ethnic order.

Looks are deceiving. The Holy Order of Mans has no connection with the Roman or Greek Catholic churches. It was founded in 1965 in San Francisco, still its headquarters, after Earl Blighton, a 65-year-old former engineer, received a "divine revelation" to establish a coed religious order.

Though members speak of "Our Lord Jesus Christ," their belief system is more occultic and Hinduistic than Christian. The phrase "uniting all faiths" is prominent on the cover of their official prospectus. They teach that Jesus was only a great human teacher who achieved "Christ-consciousness." Their document *Jesus of Nazareth* states:

> All religions have been inspired by the Cosmic Christ, the great unifying Word Principle of Good. This accounts for the similarity of all the great world teachers. The love power of the Cosmic Christ has united them even as pearls are strung on a golden thread into a single chain. (VI. 1, p. 11)

The Spiritual Counterfeits Project reports the

order is "heavily involved" in the classical occult sciences of alchemy, tarot, Kaballah, astrology, and is also studying psychic power and parapsychology. The order, the SCP believes, is "deliberately trying to put a Christian gloss on a thoroughly non-Christian content."

Despite all its strange teaching, the order has grown rapidly since its founding. A recent tabulation shows three seminaries, almost 100 missionary centers, 135 male and female priests, 600 "vowed" brothers and sisters, and at least 500 First Vow members.

The Baba Lovers movement was inspired by a gentle, hawk-nosed Indian teacher named Merwan Sheriar Irani, better known as Meher Baba, meaning "Compassionate Father." He asserted unequivocally that "I am infinite consciousness. . . . I am everything and I am beyond everything. . . . Before me was Zoroaster, Krishna, Rama, Buddha, Jesus and Mohammed. . . My present Avataric Form is the last Incarnation of this cycle of time. . . ."

Baba was born about 1894 near Bombay, India. His spiritual awakening came in college. As he recalled, he was stopped and kissed on the forehead by a saintly woman. "(She) made me experience . . . infinite bliss of self-realization." With that kiss, Baba became aware that he was the last and greatest of the divine incarnations.

Baba was a strange deity. In 1925 he opened a hospital near Meherabad, India, bringing medical care to thousands. About a year later he suddenly closed the operation, explaining only that his "external activities and commitments are only the external expression of the internal work I am doing." At this time he also stopped speaking and began communicating only through an alphabet board and hand gestures.

He first came to the West at the beginning of the Great Depression. His brooding silence and strange ways of communicating intrigued the news media and Hollywood. The Hollywood Bowl was rented for him and speculation raged about whether he would speak. But after indicating he would appear in the Bowl, he abruptly left for China, leaving his American "Lovers" holding a bag of scheduled engagements.

During each of Baba's five return trips, his "Lovers" felt he would surely speak to them. In 1962 he appeared at a special East-West assembly called "strictly for my Lovers." Over 3,000 came but his lips remained sealed.

He authorized another East-West gathering in 1969 at which he was pledged to give his last "world-renewing word. . . . When I break my silence," he promised, "the impact of my love will be universal and all life in creation will know, feel, and receive of it." But to the disappointment of his Lovers, he "dropped his body" and died before leaving India.

Today chapters of Meher Baba Lovers meet regularly on many college campuses. About three thousand persons visit the Meher Baba Spiritual Center in Myrtle Beach, South Carolina each year and reverently troop through the house in which he once lived for several months. They gaze at his robe, white underpants, locks of hair clipped at various times of his life, his alphabet board, and other relics.

The Baba Lovers issue a quarterly magazine called *The Wakener* and publish paperbacks about their departed god. And information centers are scattered across the country.

Followers, who include several show business celebrities, treasure photographs of their beloved with his off-quoted saying, "Be happy, don't worry." Enlarged pictures of the Baba hang on their walls. Smaller photos are carried close to their hearts and tiny likenesses are set in their rings.

Some of Baba's teachings are a little strange to Hindu thought. Souls come to earth from two sister planets. Those coming from one planet have 100 per cent intelligence and no love, while those migrating from the other have 75 per cent intellect and 25 per cent love. However, in the process of transmigration on earth they develop "true love."

Souls first exist on earth in stones, then move upward through metals, vegetable life, insects, reptiles, birds, and then into kangaroos, which on Baba's evolutionary scale is the first animal form. The kangaroos' front legs are small because their souls previously existed in birds. Further along the journey, souls jump from monkeys to human forms.

"In spite of their transitoriness," he revealed, "there is an unbroken continuity of life through these forms, old ones being discarded and new ones created for habitation and expression. . . . From this viewpoint," he argued, "death is an episode of minor importance.

"Love and happiness," Baba decreed, "should be the most important elements of life, and the heart should always be heeded before the mind." In other words, accept and surrender to his teachings even when they seem irrational.

Eckankar offers more new twists to the old Hindu doctrines of transmigration and reincarnation of souls. The way to self-realization is via soul travel, allowing the soul to soar free and reach higher states of consciousness.

The guru who established Eckankar in the West was Paul Twitchell, an American short story writer who first prospected for gold in New Guinea, then for eternal truth in the Orient. He claimed that the secrets of Eckankar (meaning in Sanskrit, "coworker with God") were taught to him over a quarter century by Rabazar Tarz, a Tibetan "Master" of the ancient order of Varagi and the life current (ECK) which is seen as light and heard as sound. In succeeding the Tibetan, who was reputed to have lived over 500 years, Twitchell became the 971st Living ECK Master in the Order of Varagi. His mission was to lead receptive souls back to the highest heaven, while they continued to exist in physical bodies. In short: to liberate souls from bodies.

As "The Living ECK Master," Twitchell was God's "essential expression . . . never separated from the source of true wisdom and reality." He assured ECK believers that a soul need not remain in the clutches of Karma (the cosmic law of cause and effect) and wander through eternity in a cycle of births and deaths. He would teach a path through Karma to "total awareness of God." The soul could learn to move out of its body at will, and be set free from the demands of energy, matter, and time. This would be accomplished by knowledge of Light and Sound, the essence of life flowing out of the godhead.

Twitchell's path of liberation showed ascending ovals of spiritual hierarchies, similar to ideas held by the ancient gnostics. The lowest world is the physical realm, representing science, mind, and day-to-day life as pervaded by *maya*—the illusion of reality.

He said this lower world is ruled by Kal Niranjan, the Jehovah of the Bible, but no friend of soul travelers. This Evil Power keeps souls imprisoned by the powers of *karma* and *maya*.

The object is for the disciple to break free from impediments thrown in his way by Kal and start the trip upward to the ultimate heaven (*Sugmad*). This involves rising above the mind to find a happier life, meaning simply that mind and rational thought must not be allowed to hold a soul back.

In climbing to this happier life, the Eckankar devotee must ignore Kal's enjoinder to help others. Service to fellowman, said Twitchell, is "one of Kal Niranjan's greatest traps."

The 971st Living ECK Master speaks no longer in the physical world. On September 17, 1971 Twitchell "moved up to a higher soul plane." His rod of power went to his successor, Sri Darwin Gross, at midnight, October 22 in a Las Vegas ceremony. Gross has since married Twitchell's widow.

The newest Living Master reportedly has 20,000 committed followers around the world, plus 12,000 more learners, whom he is shepherding through ECK's topsy-turvy irrational worlds.

Subud is an export from Indonesia. A Subud brochure calls it "neither a sect nor a substitute for conventional religion . . . not opposed to any denomination." Subud has no "desire, through worldly influence or power, to change or improve the world." Nor should it be "considered some kind of quick and easy cure-all for the ills of our times."

With such disclaimers, what kind of experience is Subud?

Members of local Subud groups meet usually twice a week for *Latihan,* an Indonesian word for exercise, which they describe as "a way of worshiping God . . . received from within," an experience in which participants mysteriously make contact with "higher energies."

Latihan is not open to the general public. Candidates for membership in Subud may only sit outside the room where Latihan is being carried on. Approved members are required to be over legal age or to have parental consent.

What can the candidates hear? Jacob Needleman mentions some of the sounds in his book *The New Religions:*

> At full blast, the Latihan may sound like nothing so much as jungle animals, or maniacal, savage rites, or an eerie convocation of demons and banshees. At other times it seems a deeply religious choir, or a joyous raucous celebration, a Corybantic frenzy, or a madhouse. It is, in a sense, all of these, yet none of them. There may be sudden breathtaking harmonies; a sweet fragment of melody; or deep-throated sobbing.

What happens to the participants? A Subud veteran reports: "During the Latihan, the mind, the heart, the will, and the desires are each rendered more or less inactive." Presumably, this opens the Subud communicant to envelopment by higher energies, which lead him through a process of purification in which he may not be fully in control of earthly faculties.

Strange stories have circulated about the results

of Latihan. One man was rumored to have died from unknown causes after the experience. But other Subud participants have been miraculously healed of body ailments. The founder has himself warned his followers not to try the experience too often.

The mysteries surrounding Subud have probably made the movement more alluring. The group does not pass out literature or witness on the street. Inquiring reporters have been given the cold shoulder.

Subud is said to be active in about 70 countries, with around 60 centers in the U.S. supported by some 2,000 faithful adherents.

The founder is Muhammad Subuh, known to Subud admirers as *Bapak,* an Indonesian title of respect meaning "father." Bapak was born into a Muslim family in 1901 and as a youth sought spiritual truth from various teachers. His Latihan meeting with "higher energies" came in 1925. Several years later he was "selected" to transmit the experience to others. So the story goes.

Bapak brought Subud to England in 1957. From there it spread across Europe and to the United States. The "experience" is apparently very loosely organized. "Helpers" personally selected by the founder direct centers where Latihan is held. Bapak stops in occasionally on his world tours.

Soft-spoken and bespectacled, Bapak is not known for boasting. Neither he nor his helpers make many demands. Disciples are not required to quit their jobs and join a commune. They may continue attending their regular churches if they wish.

Because of its low profile and emphasis upon personal freedom of members, Subud may seem harmless, even beneficial, to some Westerners. But others see Subud as a man-made religion designed to lead the spiritually blind and naive into dangerous paths.

Zen, which is attracting tens of thousands of Westerners, is even more puzzling to the uninitiated than Subud. Zen, says Huston Smith in *The Religions of Man,* is "a world of bewildering dialogues, obscure conundrums, stunning paradoxes, flagrant contradictions, and abrupt *non sequiturs,* all carried off in the most urbane, cheerful, and innocent style."

Before invading the illogical world of Zen, we should take a brief look at its parent, Buddhism.

Buddhism was founded in southern Nepal in 563 B.C. by Siddhartha Gautama, who at 29 had abandoned his wife and infant son to seek religious truth. For discovering why mankind was plagued with suffering and how seekers could escape to a better life, he was called Buddha, meaning "Enlightened One."

Buddha's revelation copied heavily from Hinduism. Existence is a continuing cycle of death and rebirth. A person's well-being in life is determined by *karma*—the effect of behavior in the soul's previous existences. One may be freed from the cycle of pain and suffering by breaking from worldly things.

This could be accomplished by following a self-denying "noble eightfold path": (1) Know the truth, (2) Intend to resist evil, (3) Say nothing to hurt others, (4) Respect life, morality, and property, (5) Hold only a job that injures no one, (6) Strive to free your mind of evil, (7) Control your feelings and thoughts, (8) Practice approved forms of concentration.

When the break from worldly things was complete, one would enter into a state of peace and happiness called *nirvana*.

Zen Buddhism was inspired by Buddha's famous Flower Sermon in which instead of speaking he held up a golden lotus flower. A thousand years later Zen's legendary founder, Bodhidharma, carried the lotus idea to China. From China, Zen spread to Japan and much later was carried to the United States, where it became the rage of the sandaled set in coffeehouses from Greenwich Village to Haight Ashbury.

Zen focuses on many Buddhas—past, present, and future. It even pushes the belief that one must accept himself as the Buddha. "The Buddha is your own mind," is a popular saying.

Zen Buddhism has no God in the Christian sense. Everyone is a god because everyone is part of the Ultimate. And, as in Hinduism, there is no sin, no personal responsibility, and never any separation from the Ultimate.

Zen Buddhists, to the discomfiture of more conventional Buddhists, care little for Buddhist Scriptures. In fact Zen doesn't care for any holy writings. Each person is to seek answers within himself.

Oddly, Zen enthusiasts believe in close relationships to a teacher. The best known Zen guru is Shunryu Suzuki, a seventyish Japanese, who heads up the Zen "center of gravity" in America at a California monastery. His responsibility is to help his students find within themselves solutions to what they are seeking.

What they are pursuing most is *satori*, a Zen term meaning a sudden flash of enlightenment of what holds the universe together. When one realizes satori, he will understand his own affinity with the universe.

One searches for satori by doing *zazen,* a Japanese word which roughly means "sit and meditate."

A meditator sits in the cross-legged lotus posture with the soles of his feet facing his thighs. One may meditate for hours, even days, breathing deeply from his abdomen where the deepest intuitive powers are supposed to rest.

One meditates on a *koan* spoken by great teachers. Such as: "Look at your hand. Are you in it or is it in you?" / "When the Many are reduced to the One, to what is the One to be reduced?" / "What did you look like before your ancestors were born?" / "What is the sound of one hand clapping?"

The idea is to exhaust your mind until your normal rationality is completely trapped and subdued. Then when you are no longer imprisoned by your own reason, you can break into the light of satori.

Why has Zen gained such a following in the West, where logic and rationality have been hallmarks of sensibility?

Drug use, which affects rationality, has undoubtedly led many into Zen. They seek in Zen the enlightenment they failed to find in drugs.

A second reason for Zen's appeal may be the irrationality many young people see in the straight world. A boy sees his father succeeding in his profession, while flunking in responsibilities to his health and family. The youth looks to Zen for a path to a better realization.

A third reason is that Zen is made chic and intriguing by some entertainers and academicians.

A fourth, and probably the greatest, appeal of Zen is to selfish, sinful human nature. Zen has no commandments, no morality, no responsibility to show concern for fellowman. Zen calls for complete detachment from life. Zen merely accepts the way things are and does not try to make outward changes. Zen stands in violation of the two greatest commandments of the Bible: To love (the wholly Other) God with all one's heart, soul, and mind, and one's neighbor as oneself.

Bahai, called the "religion of the future" by historian Arnold Toynbee, was presaged in Persia when Mirza Mohammed Ali announced, "Verily, I am the Bab, the Gate of God." The date, May 23, 1844 is still reverenced by Bahais as the Anniversary of the Declaration of the Bab.

The Bab added that he was only a "dewdrop" from the "limitless ocean," the herald of a Promised One. After the Bab's execution by Armenian soldiers, a wealthy nobleman named Mirza Husayn Ali pronounced himself the fulfillment of the Bab's prophecy. He took the name "Baha'u'llah," meaning "The Glory and Splendor of God." Modern Bahais regard him as their great World Teacher, the ultimate Manifestation of God.

For Bahais sin does not exist. Error is merely lack of guidance. Develop man's innate goodness, they say, and error will vanish from the world.

Their mission is to unify all divine prophets and religions and lead all mankind to reverence Baha'u'llah as the capstone of all manifestations of God.

North American Bahais have their headquarters in a dazzling temple on the Illinois shore of Lake Michigan. Membership has spiraled from less than 10,000 to more than 100,000 in the past decade. Bahai clubs are active on almost 250 U.S. college campuses. The world seat of Bahai government is in Haifa, Israel where nine male "Hands of the Cause" and a representative "Universal House of Justice" dispense instructions to the faithful.

Soka Gakkai (Value Creation Society), a Buddhist export from Japan, is led by Daisaku Ikeda, who also founded one of Japan's most powerful political parties. Ikeda is regarded by followers as a reincarnation of the god Nichiren. But he is very earthly-minded about power. "You have to have power to do anything at all meaningful," he was quoted by *Time*.

Consciousness-raising comes among Soka Gakkai faithful by repeated chanting of the *diamoku* (worship formula) in praise of the lotus sutra. Devotion is proved by making new converts. The zeal of Soka Gakkai faithful in *shakubuku* (forcible persuasion) has made them extremely controversial in Japan. Critics say their methods come close to brainwashing.

Membership has grown rapidly—from 1.3 million to 10 million since 1960. Soka Gakkai claims about 200,000 converts in the U.S.

Of the making of cults after the style of Eastern consciousness-raising of the divine within, there seems no end. Others more briefly noted:

Integral Yoga Institute, with headquarters at Pomfret Center, Connecticut, founded by Swami Satchidananda in 1966. It asserts that the body, the emotions, and the intellect can be developed to a level in which they can function healthfully and in perfect harmony with each other.

Quote sampler: "There are not many gods, there is only One. And that One has no name, no form, no place. He is everywhere—in actuality, neither he, nor she, nor it. . . . The two sides are positive and negative, light and shade. Evil also is God. If you say evil is not God, then who created evil? . . . Evil is only the absence of good. . . . The very world is an examination field. You are being tested here, purified, given experiences. You are being made fit to understand the Basic One."

The Dawn Horse Communion, fathered by Bubba Free John (alias Franklin Jones, who once studied at a Lutheran seminary). The "Communion" is the instrument through which Bubba (the "Reality, the Self, and Nature and Support of all things and all beings") "prepares and sustains" his devotees.

Quote sampler: "The Guru, even the human Guru, the one who would awaken you, is not a person. He is your very consciousness . . . the true waking state, the Heart, breaking through the force of dreaming."

The administrative center is in Middletown, California.

The Healthy Happy Holy Organization (3HO), established by Yogi Bhajan. The Yogi, Master of Kundalini Yoga and Mahan Tantric, trains teachers in "the use of breath and the mental and verbal use of sound current, or mantra, to attune the individual consciousness to the vibration of infinity."

Quote sampler: "We don't teach that *nirvana* should come after death. We believe that we should experience that state of bliss in this human body."

Headquarters of 3HO is in Los Angeles, with ashrams in other North American cities.

The count goes on.

Self-Realization Fellowship "aims to disseminate definite scientific techniques for attaining direct personal experience of God; to teach that the purpose of life is the evolution into God-Consciousness; to reveal the complete harmony between original Christianity and original Yoga and to show how to serve mankind as one's large Self." Interesting sidenote: The group claims that founder Yogananda's body remained immutable and free of decay for 20 days after his death.

Inner Light Foundation strives "to develop among all people a conscious awareness of God through a knowledge and use of the extrasensory faculties possessed by each person." It is led by Betty Bethards, a psychic and spiritual healer.

Intercosmic Center of Spiritual Associations aims "to experience one's self as the cosmic center of vibration." The founder, Dr. Rammurti S. Mishra, is also a surgeon and psychiatrist.

Church of World Messianity-Johrei features *johrei* (prayer in action), "the act of channeling the Light . . . done simply by using a focal point (a piece of rice paper with the Japanese character of Divine Light on it) to concentrate the energy. The hands are held up and the energy comes through the top of the head and out the hands."

There are many other movements that could be listed. Indeed, the number, variety, geographical spread, and growth of the Eastern religions across the United States and other Western nations is astounding. Why has the ground become so fertile in the West?

It is because "Americans have lost their roots," the Catholic Archbishop of Bangalore, India, Packiam Arokiaswany told McCandlish Phillips of the *National Courier*. American society, he said, "is like a rat which has eaten poison and burns inside, and goes around to every puddle and drinks here and drinks there, but it does not quench its thirst or stop that fire."

He defined the poisons as excesses of self-indulgence and pleasure, material comforts, immorality, and infidelity. The "puddles" are Eastern mystical practices like TM that promise relief but do not ultimately provide it.

Hare Krishna, he noted, is "practically unknown" in India. "TM is not much respected," and the Indian people "hardly know the Guru Maharaj Ji of the Divine Light Mission."

Irvine Robertson, a Moody Bible Institute faculty member who spent 12 years in India as a missionary, tends to agree. In an article for *Moody Monthly* (July-August, 1973), "The Eastern Mystics Are Out to Take You In," he declared:

Why do the Eastern religions find so many vulnerable adherents in the U.S.? Perhaps interest in the Perennial Philosophy surges because our satiation with undisciplined self-gratification has led to frustration. Many young people, having been given everything, find no lasting satisfaction in anything. With nothing new to try, drugs and free sex having failed, some seek happiness in the esoteric, the mystical. And how gratifying to the ego to be singled out as the source of lasting peace and happiness! The do-it-yourself formula appeals more strongly than the message of repentance from sin and faith in God's Son.

7

Satan on the Loose

The Devil's Hour in San Francisco! Midnight. An organ booms in the black darkness. Sweet seductive incense wafts across the ritual chamber. Red and black candles flicker, and now six hooded men can be seen bobbing their heads a few steps in front of the altar-fireplace. They are bowing to a red-haired girl who lies nude on a fur rug.

Suddenly another tall, hooded figure steps from the shadows and rings a loud bell. Then lifting his robed arm above his face like the villain from Faust, he leads in a litany of invocation: "Abaddon, Apollyon, Asmodeus, Moloch." The names of Satan from ancient pagan cultures roll off his tongue and leap across the room. And the priests before the altar and Satan worshipers standing about the room respond: "Shemhamforash! Hail Satan! Hail Satan! Hail!"

It happens regularly. Prayers and chants rise to Satan and lesser demons. Curses are hurled on enemies. Blasphemies are thrown at Christianity.

Not by crazed drug addicts, but by worshipers who afterward melt into the stream of ordinary society.

Across the bay in a futuristic apartment complex on a curving lake, a related ritual is about to begin. It is the eve of a full moon and in the softly-lit room about 30 naked young men and women hold hands and cavort in a circle dance, first rotating clockwise, then counterclockwise, then romping snake-like through the rooms of the apartment, with participants stopping occasionally to plant a quick kiss on nearby lips—the witch's greeting.

Someone starts a litany of praise to the chief witch of the coven and others take it up until the apartment is pulsating with sound. The circle begins symbolically closing as a young girl chants and prances behind with a sword pointing downward. There is the elevation of a male and female witch to the positions of priest and priestess, the passing of a cup of wine, more recitations to strange deities, and the ritual is over.

Then after melon and cookies, the participants all put their clothes on and go home.

Worship of Satan in black masses, and of ancient pagan gods in coven rituals, occurs regularly in San Francisco and other major cities. Tens of thousands of Americans, some with advanced academic degrees, are known to be into Satanism, witchcraft, voodoo, and varieties of black or white magic. A reported 50,000 have signed up for a correspondence course in the occult. A witches' magazine claims 10 million practicing adherents in the U.S. (an exaggeration, no doubt, but still alarming). The German Medical Information Service estimates 10,000 Germans participate in occultic rites. And in England there are said to be 30,000 active witches.

Most people represented in these statistics are probably not 100 per cent committed to the occult; they are dabbling, experimenting, seeking knowledge and thrills to enliven daily existence. It is those who have gone deeper into the dark labyrinth of demonic realms that have suffered untold psychic damage, and in some cases, physical harm.

Take the sad story of young Richard Lucas (anonymous name), the rebellious son of a Southern Baptist minister. While browsing in his father's library, he came across some books on demonism. That night while thinking about what he had read, he heard yells and screams coming from outside. He ran to the door and found no one. Then, back in bed, he heard the cries again.

He tried painting white crosses on the walls and door of his room. The noises got more horrendous. Three weeks later he painted over the crosses and surrendered himself to the tormenting powers.

After moving into his own apartment, he combed local bookstores for everything he could find about the occult and Satanism. Among the books he read was the *Satanic Bible,* written by Anton La Vey, credited with founding the Satan church movement in the U.S. One commandment intrigued him: "If someone bothers you, ask him to stop. If he does not stop, destroy him!" One reason for his previous rebellion had been his mother's admonition that it was wrong to fight. La Vey's encouragement was a shot of adrenalin.

Richard's wages as an apprentice electrician were not enough to pursue his new hobby and to maintain the narcotics habit he had picked up. When several checks bounced, he split to Daytona Beach, Florida. Broke, and in a frenzy for more dope, he pledged his soul to the devil for money. Within the week $500 came in the mail. To keep his promise, he made a ritual chamber in his dingy basement apartment, sketching demonic symbols on the wall and painting an old workbench black for an altar.

A young couple attracted to Satanism began worshiping with him in the basement. Sometimes they'd just burn a leaf from the Bible and sit and try to mentally conjure up a demon. Others began coming, and within a few months they had a sizable congregation.

Their perversions came to light when the body of a 17-year-old initiate was discovered, beaten to a pulp. Police first thought he had been "sacrificed" in the ritual. Then evidence was found that indicated a grudge murder by some of the group.

Young Lucus claimed he had been stoned on drugs and couldn't remember anything from the time they took the victim downstairs. Still he refused to be reconciled to his parents. He vowed to continue Satan worship in hopes of receiving a reward he called "freedom."

The Daytona Beach murder is only one of a series of tragedies that appear to be related to Satanism and/or witchcraft. Consider:

• The body of a Springfield, New Jersey teenager—a good girl, straight, and very religious, according to those who knew her—was discovered in a quarry. Makeshift wooden crosses were staked out around the body. Family members and her Assemblies of God pastor suspect Satanists. Whether true or not, a large "grotto" branch of the Church of Satan is active in the area, with members carrying plastic cards identifying themselves as "Citizens of the Infernal Empire." Many members are believed to be older teenagers; area librarians say they can't keep books on witchcraft on the shelves.

• Kim Brown, a long-haired, 22-year-old Miami Satanist, was convicted of manslaughter for stabbing a 62-year-old man to death, something she "enjoyed" doing. She credits her light prison sentence of seven years to the intercession of Satan and continues to hold rituals to the devil in prison.

• In Vineland, New Jersey two local youths killed a third, Patrick Michael Newell, at the victim's behest. Presumably, young Newell persuaded his friends that if they murdered him Satan would return him to earth as the leader of 40 legions of demons.

• A Kentucky warlock, who administers sobriety tests for a police department, brags about avenging himself on some former cult members who got him "excommunicated" from a grotto. After he and his wife pronounced a curse and burned wax images of each, two were injured at work, two were shot by an estranged husband, and a fifth left the church after an internal squabble.

• A 14-year-old girl in Fort Lauderdale, Florida was married in a Satanic ceremony and forced to have sexual intercourse with five young men on her wedding night. Similar stories of sexual perversion circulate in other cities.

• In California over 100 murders have been tied to occultish rites. Los Angeles police speculate Satanists may have murdered a school teacher and later desecrated her grave and dismembered her corpse. The Los Angeles police regularly hear stories of dogs, cats, and other animals being sacrificed in witchery rites. One informant described how a dog was killed and his blood mixed with LSD and drunk by participants.

• Convicted mass-murderer Charles Manson told a reporter all his women were witches and that he was the devil. Those he sent to kill Sharon Tate and her house guests called themselves "Satan's slaves."

• A San Diego coed coldly admitted she had been ordered by Satan to hack off a male student's leg.

• Dr. Hardat Sukhdeo, a Miami physician, reports up to 900 persons a month coming to a local hospital to have evil spirits driven from their bodies.

• Mrs. Norma Horner, a Houston mother, claims the *Satanic Bible* influenced her 13-year-old son and 12-year-old daughter to aid an older youth in kidnapping and killing a 61-year-old San Antonio woman.

Yet despite publicity of these and many other horrifying incidents, most Americans probably do not grasp the seriousness of the revival of Satanism and witchcraft. Talk shows continue to feature witches. Master Satanist Anton La Vey appeared on the Johnny Carson show. Wearing a horned hood and showing off a ceremonial magic sword, he casually described how his church used a naked woman to symbolize the pleasures of the flesh.

Still, liberal avant-garde ministers and theologians continue to snicker at the reality of Satan and evil spirits. For example, the University of Chicago's Martin Marty wrote in the *Christian Century,* "Yes, the devil is relevant as always: to explain what's wrong with the other guy, with your opponents, or with yourself, in case you don't want to take responsibility in the world."

Marty passed off a pronouncement by Pope Paul as mere "devil-talk," dropped "casually onto a scene where theologians have had enough trouble with God-talk." The Pope had called the devil a "perfidious and astute charmer who manages to insinuate himself into us by way of the senses, of fantasy, of concupiscence, of utopian logic, or disorderly contacts."

Bible-believing Protestants have never had much trouble acknowledging supernatural evil powers, directed by Satan. The devil was so real to Martin Luther that he once threw a bottle of ink at where he imagined the Evil One to be standing.

Satan is called a variety of things in the Bible, including accuser, adversary, slanderer, Abaddon, Apollyon, Beelzebub, Belial, deceiver of the whole world, great dragon, god of this world, murderer, prince of the power of the air, and tempter. Some of these names are used by Satan worshipers in their invocations to the devil.

The origin of the devil is not spelled out in detail in the Bible. Indications are that he was once an exalted spiritual being, commanding vast legions of other spirit beings who joined his ill-fated rebellion against God. After his fall, he was allowed to continue limited warfare against the Creator and His loyal angels. Earth became the stage where Satan and His evil powers struggle relentlessly against their opposites. The minds and hearts of humans, created in God's image but corrupted by sin, are the battleground.

The biblical idea of Satan is poles apart from the occultish, Hinduistic doctrine that Satan is contained within the cosmogony of the Godhead. Satan, according to the Bible, stands apart from and in warfare against God. His activities are truly evil, not fancied. He deceives, seduces, snatches away the Word of God from impressionable minds, obscures and blinds minds from the true Light, plants his counterfeits and spies among God's people, and even appears as an "angel of light" by presenting his apostles of deceit as messengers of truth.

The Bible predicts that ultimately the curtain will ring down on the conflict of the ages. Satan's time will have run out, and he will be banished in final defeat to perdition with all of his subjects.

Even those who dismiss the biblical treatment of Satan as "mythical" must concede that Satan worship and witchcraft have a long history. Witches don't like to be associated with Satan because of the notorious atrocities laid at the feet of devil worshipers. But the two groups are hard to separate. The best that can be said for witchcraft is that it is a handmaiden of Satanism.

The word witch is from the old English word *wican*, meaning "to yield." A witch is one who yields to the practice of sorcery, which is the use of supernatural powers to work evil. (Some witches claim to use their powers only for good, as we shall discuss later.) Generally, witchcraft is simply doing the devil's work while Satanism involves direct worship of the ruler of evil forces.

There are chilling references to witchcraft throughout ancient literature. Witchery and divination (the attempt to obtain secret knowledge) are condemned in the Old Testament. "Thou shalt not suffer a witch to live," we read in Exodus 22:18. Harsh? Yes, but the severity is blunted by the connection between witches and the pagan gods worshiped by neighbor tribes. The Ammonites, for instance, worshiped the god Moloch with sex orgies and ritual sacrifice of children.

Witchcraft was intimately associated with religious worship long before Christianity came to Europe. When the Catholic church took control, prelates at first ignored the practice as a harmless delusion of ignorant peasants. When the Black Plague swept across Europe, however, the masses turned back to the old charms and incantations in hopes of survival. The Roman hierarchy became alarmed and in the late 15th century Pope Innocent VIII condemned witchcraft and forbade Catholics to consult with witches.

Witch hunting became a mania. Prosecutors looked for "devil's marks" on a woman's body—moles, birthmarks, and other blemishes where a pin would not cause pain. In another test a suspected woman's arms and legs were tied and she was thrown into deep water. If she floated, she was branded a witch. If she sank, she was declared innocent. Historians estimate that from 1484 to 1782 church-state prosecutors killed upward of a million women for witchcraft, with many tortured until they confessed to being witches simply to escape further torment. Joan of Arc was one of those burned at the stake for witchery.

The Satanist Black Mass was viewed as the most infamous blasphemy of Christianity. In the practice the symbols and rituals of Christianity were reversed. The crucifix was hung upside down, the altar was covered with black instead of white cloth and adorned by a naked woman (a virgin preferred). Hymns were sung backward, communion was partaken with wafers and real blood in mockery of the Catholic doctrine of transubstantiation, sexual perversions were practiced, and sometimes an animal or a child was sacrificed. At the close of a ceremony, the leader, sometimes a defrocked priest, pronounced curses, and invited Catholics present to renounce their faith and pledge allegiance to Satan as lord.

In the late 17th century Satanists tried to topple the throne of France. The scandal began when King Louis XIV's mistress asked a Satanist priestess to help her advance in the king's favor. The priestess held a Black Mass in which an infant was sacrificed and a blood wafer prepared for the king as a love potion. After three Black Masses brought no success, the high priestess plotted to poison the king.

But the plot was discovered. When confronted, the priestess confessed to having sacrificed, burned, and buried in her garden over 2500 infants. More shock waves swept France and all of Europe when further investigation implicated several Catholic priests and other prominent Frenchmen.

The public uproar crippled the Satanist movement and kept die-hard practitioners fleeing from one town to another.

European colonists brought both the practice and fear of witchcraft to America. Colonial preachers such as Cotton Mather whipped public anxiety into an abusive frenzy. About the time of the Paris scandal, the colony of Massachusetts executed 20 persons as witches and imprisoned 150 others.

Both in Europe and America terrible injustices were perpetrated in the name of fighting Satan. These are reported in school histories, while, unfortunately, the crimes of Satanists and witches are romanticized.

After the Massachusetts trials in colonial America, Satanism and witchcraft did not flower again in America until after World War II. The chief "horticulturist" of modern Satanism is Anton Szandor La Vey, the high priest of the bellwether Church of Satan in San Francisco.

How La Vey became the "Billy Graham" of Satanism is an interesting story. As a young man, he played the organ in the carnival that accompanied the Clyde Beatty Circus. On Saturday nights he would observe men lusting after striptease artists. The next morning, when performing for a tent church, he would see many of the same customers begging forgiveness at a bench altar. Then the next Saturday night he would see them back in the burlesque show. "I knew then that the Christian church thrives on hypocrisy, and that man's carnal nature will win out!" he said later.

La Vey's belief in the power of carnality was strengthened when he worked as a photographer for the San Francisco police department. After three years of seeing bloody results of the dark side of human nature, he decided to start a church in honor of Satan. Tall, with shaved head, smooth skin, impeccably trimmed beard, and small piercing eyes, he wore a Roman collar and a Satanic medallion on a silver chain around his neck. In an area known for imaginative depravity, he became an instant celebrity.

His newly published *Satanic Bible* was a sensation.

"Why should not I hate mine enemies?" he argued in it. "If I love them, does it not place me at their mercy?"

"Are we not all predatory animals by instinct?

If humans ceased wholly from preying upon each other, could they continue to exist?"

"He who turns the other cheek is a cowardly dog."

"You should act upon your natural instincts. . . . It's a lot of fun to do things you are not supposed to do."

· He even included a number of Satanist "Beatitudes." Among them,

"Cursed are the meek, for they shall inherit the yoke!"

"Blessed are the strong, for they shall possess the earth!"

"Cursed are the 'lambs of God' for they shall be bled whiter than snow!"

La Vey is a showman who knows how to grab the attention of a sensation-craving public. But he disclaims connection with Satanist congregations and worshipers who commit atrocities. He claims his church members are just ordinary folks who believe devotion to Satan will help them be more successful in society. He decries drug use and says he does not like to perform a Black Mass.

He has on occasions pronounced ritual curses. One involved actress Jayne Mansfield, then a member of his church. When La Vey heard that the actress' lawyer boyfriend, Sam Brody, hated the group because of her involvement, he reportedly predicted, "You'll be dead in a year." Within a year, Brody died in an auto crash near New Orleans. Sitting beside him, Miss Mansfield also died—she was decapitated.

Sybil Leek, the best known witch, tries even harder than La Vey to project an image of respectability. Besides being a practicing witch who claims to be almost six centuries old, through a chain of incarnations, she sells antiques, writes a newspaper column, holds séances, and makes pronouncements on astrology.

Respectable witches like Sybil Leek even have their own journals. One is appropriately called *The New Broom*. The first issue bragged that "our numbers increase with every waxing moon," but complained that "too much is being badly written about us."

The *New Broom* defines a witch as

A person who worships a pantheon whose chief deity is the goddess who is known by many names. The goddess and her consort are worshiped and celebrated in many rituals which may differ slightly or radically from one coven to the next. . . . Nevertheless, every witch believes herself to be a part of Nature, not apart from it, and because of her belief, strives to become totally attuned with Nature and Nature's pulses and rhythms.

Some witches practice nude while others prefer to worship and work robed. Initiations vary as do methods of advancement. The multiplicity of viewpoints has, on occasion, sparked a kind of our-ritual-is-better-than-your-ritual bickering . . . but the diversity does fill a need of each Seeker.

This is not a claim that witches are "paragons of virtue." An angry witch may be quite capable of incapacitating anyone who has provoked her. Bitterness between witches or factions does crop up with sometimes unpleasant results. Spellcasting can fail, experiments can get them into trouble, and disobedience to a high priestess can make calamity for many.

Not a word about Satan or an invocation to the devil.

Modern witches claim to follow the "Old Religion" of nature worship, which flourished in Europe before Catholic missionaries arrived. In this Old Religion the "Mother Goddess" represented the female forces in nature. Her companion, the "Horned God," stood for the male principle.

Hans Holzer is a scholarly writer, sympathetic to modern witchcraft. He concedes that "black" witches may see themselves as aligned with evil Satanic powers, but says "white" witches, who are in the great majority, cast spells only for good. He also claims, quite correctly, that neither black nor white witchery follows the Satanist ritual in mocking Christian worship.

Holzer and other authorities agree that witchcraft is a celebration of sensual appetites, a doing of what comes naturally.

Covens vary in the way they ritualize sensuality. One east coast group takes off their clothes and bathes in saltwater to become purified. Then they dance naked in a circle and chant, drink wine, and read from witchcraft's "bible," *The Book of Shadows.*

An initiate to this coven is led naked into a circle of witches and wizards. The high priest delivers a charge to worship the powers of nature represented in the female principle of fertility and the male principle of procreation. The new member is then scourged, helped to her feet, and given the witches' fivefold kiss on the feet, the knees, the genitals, the breasts, and the lips.

Sexual intercourse, the joining of the male and female principle, may be celebrated at this time, or it may be scheduled for an advanced ceremony sometime later.

None of the essentials of witchcraft appear to have changed. What is striking is that after hundreds of years underground, witchcraft has become popular in modern avant-garde, permissive circles of entertainment and education. How-to books on black magic, witchery, and Satanist rituals are now in most libraries, sold in regular bookstores, and offered through occult book clubs.

Witchcraft, Satanism, and demonism have become hot themes for television and movies. The popular "Bewitched," now syndicated, is considered only a harmless sitcom by most families. More ominously, "devil" movies, starting with *Rosemary's Baby* are proved box office hits. After the success of *The Omen* in which the biblical Antichrist is portrayed as a young child, a dozen more devil movies were planned. One promises to give viewers "nightmares forever." Ted Tanen, executive vice-president of MCA production company, says, "Devil movies are the current staple. They've even eclipsed the Western."

The wave of occultic films and TV dramas has doubtless been inspired by sensational stories about Satanism and witchery, as well as by the success of such apocalyptic Christian best-sellers as Hal Lindsey's *The Late Great Planet Earth*. These films, in turn, are undoubtedly creating more interest in occultism. Unfortunately, some viewers are tempted to try what they see on the screen. Or they become so involved emotionally that it affects their behavior. Incidents of adults, even parents, killing children who they believe have been possessed by the devil, are now occurring. Some of the killers say they have been influenced by recent movies about devil-possessed children.

And courses in witchcraft and Satanism are even being taught in public high schools at the expense of the taxpayer.

Item: Tremper High School, Kenosha, Wisconsin announced a new literature course, "Literature of the Supernatural." A teacher explained that it wasn't "designed to be a course in witchcraft or occultism, but . . . I think the course will appeal to kids who are interested in this sort of thing." (Apparently many students are interested in Wisconsin; a University of Wisconsin poll found 23% of 231 college juniors and seniors believing in witchcraft.)

Item: Three public high schools in Fresno, California taught "Literature of the Supernatural," and a Satanist Black Mass was celebrated in one school as a part of the study, with students required to participate.

Item: The administration of the Bryant Junior High School in Minneapolis sent the following letter to a list of parents:

Your child is enrolled in the Supernatural course at Bryant Junior High School. I have decided to mail this letter at the beginning of the semester in order that you may be more familiar with what will be expected of your child from the start.

Our first unit is superstition and requires gathering a list of superstitions, and studying the origin of many common superstitions. A paper will be assigned. The second unit covers mythical and semimythical characters, such as vampires, werewolves, Frankenstein, ghosts and witches. Your child will view movies and discuss origins,

truths, and myths. Also, there will be a séance
conducted.

If finances permit, we may have a guest
speaker, either a medium or a witch.

Parents' groups and Christian clergy have protested strongly the inclusion of such material in
public school curriculums. In Culver City, California, for example, the local chapter of American
Christians in Education (ACE) lambasted their
school board for approving junior high study of
"Literature of the Supernatural" despite "expert
testimony on the harm and dangers that the occult
causes to the students' physical, spiritual, and psychological well-being. . . . [The course] is only presenting the occultic side of the supernatural and not
the theistic side. Therefore, this course is indoctrinating and not educating the students."

In a separate protest, Culver City's Mayor Richard
E. Pachtman declared, "We the citizens of Culver
City are convinced that our children can have a
complete and enriching educational experience
without knowing the gory and lurid details of
witches and child sacrifice."

Interest and participation in witchcraft and
Satanism continues unabated. Many Christians see
the unholy revival as a sign of the impending Second Coming of Christ as predicted in the New
Testament. Many secularists view the movement as
an unhealthy and abnormal foreshadowing of the
degeneration and disintegration of society.

But this does not explain why such practices,
long abhorrent to the majority of Americans, are
so appealing, especially to young people.

Researchers find a variety of pulls to Satanism

and witchcraft: morbid curiosity, rebellion against upbringing, search for new sex thrills, desire for hidden powers, and, for some perverted souls, opportunities to practice violence and sadism.

Dr. Joyce Brothers, in a column titled: "Mysticism: Reasoning Out the Occult," cited three views of why people are attracted to such things as witchcraft.

• Essayist Edmund Wilson: "The longing for mystical experience always seems to manifest itself in periods of social confusion when political progress is blocked: As soon as we feel that our world has failed us, we try to find evidence for another world."

• "Some theologians . . . [are] saying that ritualistic religions have not provided the healing to the human spirit that people expect. As a result, both young and old have turned to the mythical spirits of ancient times for solace or for a sense of energy."

• Mortimer R. Feinberg, a professor of psychology: "The closer we get to a controlled, totally predictable society, the more man becomes fearful of the consequences. Interest in mysticism is a regression to a childlike state of mind."

Perhaps a more telling explanation can be found in Paul's Epistle to the Roman Christians, who lived in the midst of flourishing witchcraft and Satanism:

They knew all the time that there is a God, yet they refused to acknowledge Him as such, or to thank Him for what He is or does. Thus they became fatuous in their argumentations, and plunged their silly minds still further into the dark. Behind a facade of "wisdom" they became just fools, fools who would exchange the glory of the immortal God for an image of a mortal man, or of creatures that run or fly or crawl. They gave up God: and therefore God gave them up—to be the playthings of their own foul desires in dishonoring their own bodies. . . .

Moreover, since they considered themselves too high and mighty to acknowledge God, He allowed them to become the slaves of their degenerate minds, and to perform unmentionable deeds. They became filled with wickedness, rottenness, greed and malice; their minds became steeped in envy, murder, quarrelsomeness, deceitfulness and spite. They became whisperers-behind-doors, stabbers-in-the-back, God-haters; they overflowed with insolent pride and boastfulness, and their minds teemed with diabolical invention. They scoffed at duty to parents; they mocked at learning, recognized no obligations of honor, lost all natural affection, and had no use for mercy. More than this—being well aware of God's pronouncement that all who do these things deserve to die, they not only continued their own practices, but did not hesitate to give their thorough approval to others who did the same (1:21-25; 28-29, PH.).

8

The Mind Business

A generation ago they might have been selling sleek, high-finned gas guzzlers, deep pile carpeting, encyclopedias, or 10 easy steps for climbing the corporate ladder. Today they are peddling consciousness expansion, emotional liberation, mind control, advanced sensory perception, deeper awareness—in short, a new you.

Hucksters or mind researchers, supersalesmen or psychotherapists, greed merchants or humanistic gurus—no matter what they're called, they're netting converts with an evangelistic zeal akin to the revivalism of the 18th century. Says *Newsweek* in a recent seven-page cover article "Getting Your Head Together": the "consciousness revolution . . . may well turn out to be this century's version of colonial America's Great Awakening. As philosopher Jacob Needleman puts it, from 'getting what you want,' the idea of happiness has been transformed into 'changing what you are.'"

Philosophically, the corporate mind business represents a marriage between the old Eastern religions and the new Western psychotherapies. Man is basically good. The god principle is wholly within. Salvation comes in freeing yourself from old hang-ups and inhibitions and opening yourself to new revelation, new experience, and new rapprochement with the fundamental powers of nature.

Consciousness-raising has existed in the West at least since early New England transcendentalists dabbled with "Yankee Hindooism." But the market wasn't exploited until after mind-expanding hallucinatory drugs left a stream of wrecked psyches in the '60s. Experimental psychologists searched for nonchemical means of altering consciousness and found the Eastern yoga techniques sensational.

First at the starting line was the Esalen Institute, founded by Michael Murphy, who had studied yoga in India. Murphy and his idealistic colleagues thought the new consciousness technique might lift humanity out of the materialistic gutter. They were disappointed when Esalen was absorbed into the Association for Humanistic Psychology, which included anyone with a method for mind elevation and a $35 annual membership fee. (At a recent AHP conference in Atlantic City—1600 delegates in 135 workshops—some delegates apparently tried mind-altering gimmicks outside of conventional morality. Hundreds cavorted nude at a late night pool party while others held hands and gazed at erotic films.)

The AHP does little more than provide articles for psychological journals. It is the independent free-lancers who are gaining the followers. Unlike the cults whose main appeal is to young people, the mind marketeers are signing up affluent customers with established incomes, people who can pay and pay—and pay.

We have already dealt with TM, which is getting a big piece of the multimillion dollar pie Americans are dishing up for mind-altering. Now we will look at two distinctly Americanized innovations in the mind market: Scientology and Erhard Seminars Training (est).

Scientology is the revelatory brainchild of Lafayette Ron Hubbard, who describes himself as an engineer, author, and philosopher. Born in Nebraska in 1911, Hubbard spent his teen years in the Orient, then returned to the U.S. for two years of college. For a time he signed his name with a Ph.D. from Sequoia University (once called the College of Drugless Healing), but now uses D.Scn., which stands for Doctor of Scientology.

After serving as a U.S. naval officer in World War II, Hubbard turned to writing science fiction. In May 1950, his exposition of a strange system of psychotherapy called "Dianetics" appeared in *Astounding Science Fiction.* That same year his book *Dianetics: The Modern Science of Mental Health* was published and became a quick best-seller. Hubbard called his new program "a milestone for man comparable to the discovery of fire and superior to the wheel and the arch."

Hubbard divided the mind into two compartments: the analytic (the conscious, rational mind) and the reactive (the storehouse of unpleasant memories—"engrams").

Engrams, he said, were recorded on the protoplasm of cells as the results of acute pain or emotional shocks. They were the "single source of aberrations and psychosomatic ills." Later he would teach that engrams may be carried over from pre-existent lives.

Treatment of human ills, he said, involved exposing and erasing engrams until the analytic mind gained dominance over the reactive mind.

Dianetics flared as a fad in the pop psychology field for a while, then began fading. Hubbard hung on, saying his new healing science was useful for treating "all inorganic mental ills and all organic psychosomatic ills, with assurance of complete cure in unselected cases."

When the market didn't respond, in 1955 Hubbard wrapped his ideas in a religious package by establishing the Founding Church of Scientology in Washington, D.C. *Time* would later recall that in 1949 Hubbard had joked to an authors' convention, "Writing for a penny a word is ridiculous. If a man really wanted to make a million dollars, the best way would be to start his own religion."

Hubbard built his theological base on deities he called *thetans*. They were eternal, all-knowing, all-seeing, free from all physical laws and exempt from *karma* cause and effect relationships.

Thetans, Hubbard revealed, had gotten together to create the Material-Energy-Space-Time (M-E-S-T) universe outside of their realm. The eternal ones decided to enter the M-E-S-T universe by incarnating themselves in plants and animals and then reincarnating into higher species as these life forms died. With the advance of time and evolution, the thetans picked up nasty engrams, as a ship might accumulate barnacles. By the time man had evolved, they had forgotten their divinity.

Hubbard's church took on the terminology and

trappings of a new Christian denomination. Crosses were displayed on cloth-covered altars. Cassocked and collared "ministers" held Sunday services; performed christenings, marriages, and funerals; and counseled "parishioners." The founder, of course, provided spiritual guidebooks for the ministers to follow in relating the church's theology to ceremonies. During a christening, for instance, a minister introduced the thetan to its new body as well as to the parents and godparents.

Hubbard may have been joking about making a million by starting a new religion, but the success of his Church of Scientology is no joke. He now claims three million members in the U.S. and another million worldwide. Annual gross income, mostly from "counseling" fees, is estimated to be above $70 million.

Hubbard, thrice married, reportedly receives 10 per cent of all fees collected, and *Time* says he has boasted to friends of having $7 million tucked away in numbered Swiss bank accounts. He spends much of his time sailing on his luxury yacht with a crew of 200 sailors and students. Many of the crew members are believed to have signed billion-year contracts to work for their mentor without pay.

The counseling or "auditing" process is the key technique. The beginning Scientologist, called a "preclear," sits across a cloth-covered table from his "auditor." A cross looms beside them and between them is the controversial E-meter, which functions as a sort of lie detector. The "preclear" grasps two light metal cans connected to the meter, dials, and needle of the device. The auditor asks questions, some of a highly personal nature, and checks the preclear's reaction on the E-meter. The E-meter simply reveals changes in the electrical resistance of the skin.

The auditor probes for painful past experiences or traumas which may have left engrams. A regular question is, "Tell me something you wouldn't mind forgetting." A lie or failure to tell all the truth will show up on the E-meter. The auditor keeps probing until assured the truth has come out and the related engram erased. Says Hubbard: "The E-meter is never wrong. It sees all; it knows all. It tells everything."

As engrams are contacted and erased from his reactive mind, the student progresses through eight grades of clearness, paying from $15 to $35 an hour for each session. Total expenditures may run into the thousands of dollars by the time he passes the eighth grade and moves into the final clear, an accomplishment attained by less than 5,000 Scientologists.

Beside being a successful religious enterprise, Scientology is also extremely controversial. Rarely will a person knowledgable of Scientology be neutral. Thousands of members, including such celebrities as actress Karen Black and former pro-football quarterback John Brodie, praise it. Some former members, parents of present members, and many government officials roundly condemn it. Press opinion ranges from "dangerous" to "therapeutic."

The Supreme Court of Victoria, Australia banned Scientology after 160 days of hearing testimony. The court declared, "Scientology is evil; its techniques evil; its practice a serious threat to the community, medically, morally, and socially; and its adherents are sadly deluded and often mentally ill."

The justices described Scientology as the "world's largest organization of unqualified persons engaged in the practice of dangerous techniques which masquerade as mental therapy." The Australian Parliament banned the teaching, application, or advertising of Scientology in 1965. But the law was repealed in 1973 and the church now enjoys tax exemption there.

Scientology has also been bitterly fought in England. Minister of Health Kenneth Robinson reportedly charged Scientologists with directing "themselves to the weak, the unbalanced, the immature, the rootless, and the mentally and emotionally unstable." He termed their "authoritarian principles . . . a potential menace . . . to the well-being of those so deluded as to become . . . followers." England not only still refuses to grant religious status, but has removed the Hubbard College of Scientology from the approved list of educational establishments, thus denying immigration permits for foreigners to come and study Scientology at the school.

Scientology has also been in trouble with U.S. agencies but, since winning a court decision, it has enjoyed more solid status as a religion. The contested action was initiated in 1963 when Food and Drug Administration agents raided the church's Washington headquarters and seized 100 E-meters used in counseling members.

The government contended that the E-meter was worthless for treatment of any disease. Scientology claimed the instrument was a religious artifact and could no more be outlawed than could the use of holy water, icons, or a crucifix.

The FDA won the case. Scientology appealed. In

1969 a U.S. court of appeals reversed the previous decision on the principle of religious freedom and said government and medical authorities hold no jurisdiction over religious matters.

Some grieving parents, estranged from their children by Scientology, are calling for government investigation of alleged mind-changing techniques of Scientology and exploitation of young people. Mrs. Elaine Lieberman filed this testimony for the 1976 Day of Affirmation and Protest:

> We have just lived through an experience which seems more science fiction than real. Our very open, intelligent, and caring son joined Scientology to improve his studies and his abilities. It advertises heightened awareness and making a sane world. The ideas seem fine. Instead, in four months he became irrational and robotlike. He was put in a trance-like state. He was convinced that Scientology had all the answers and he became a slave to a totalitarian system that went against all his previous beliefs. It uses psuedo-psychiatric techniques and thru auditing and hypnotism one confesses all fears and guilts plus hallucinates past lives. If you want to get out they use your confessions as blackmail. Also, you are threatened and told to "disconnect" with all people trying to interfere with your Scientology training. They are masters of mind manipulation or brainwashing.
>
> The cost of the training averages $5,000 to $20,000. How this has church status is beyond belief!

The strongest and most sustained opposition has come from the medical profession. The American

Medical Association's journal *Today's Health* called Scientology a "dangerous cult." Dr. Joseph A. Sabatier, Jr., head of the AMA committee on quackery, noted that "Scientology is being sold to youth like a mental patent medicine." But the AMA, the American Psychiatric Association, and several other public and private agencies say they are blocked in pressing any attack because of Scientology's religious status.

The controversy and criticism has engendered widespread media attention, mostly unfavorable to Scientology. Hubbard's church, *Time* observed, "has tended toward defensiveness bordering on paranoia, filing scores of libel suits on the slightest provocation."

Scientology's quoted response from a spokesman: "We are not a turn-the-other-cheek religion."

In 1974 a *St. Louis Post-Dispatch* team published a five-part series, one of the most ambitious media projects on Scientology to date. In sending copies to a fellow newsman on another paper, one of the writers noted that since publication "the local and national [Scientology] boys have rattled a lot of sabres at us," but since the newspaper's attorney had read all the copy before publication there was no concern. Shortly afterward a multimillion dollar suit was filed against the paper.

Scientology has also sued or threatened to bring legal action against dozens of other publications, including the *San Francisco Chronicle,* the *Washington Post,* and the *Los Angeles Times.* Interestingly, the *Times'* closely guarded morgue has twice lost packets of clippings on Scientology. Religion writer Russell Chandler now files material on the subject under another name.

Bitter ex-Scientologists have served as sources for critical articles. Robert Kaufman, a New York musician, according to the *St. Louis Post-Dispatch*, claims he was driven close to insanity and suicide after spending $8,000 on advanced Scientology programming. He wrote in his book *Inside Scientology* that the system is dangerous to the human spirit because it is so outrageously absolutist.

Another author of a book on Scientology, free-lancer Paulette Cooper, claims the organization has wiretapped her telephone, had her watched and followed, visited her late at night, subjected her to libel litigation, and had her publisher threatened and sued. She has filed a $15.4 million damage suit in the California State Supreme Court.

For every opponent, Scientology has hundreds of testimonials from students and members who declare Hubbard's system has freed them from emotional and, in some instances, physical problems through its techniques to help them live a richer, fuller life.

At least one prominent newsman, who is himself writing a book on Scientology, believes Hubbard's organization has been maligned by the psychiatric profession. In bringing out the "other side" of the FDA-Scientology controversy, William Willoughby probably contributed to the court of appeals decision that established Scientology as a "religion."

Willoughby, Religion Editor of the *Washington Star-News* and also an ordained evangelical minister, contended that the FDA had been unfairly persecuting Scientology. His "interpretative" article precipitated other stories by the *New York Times* and the Associated Press that presented the Scientology case as a test of religious freedom.

Outside the court chambers on the day of the appeals trial, Willoughby was assailed by an FDA attorney for doing the government organization a "disservice." Other officials charged, he reported later, "that I was 'taken in' by the Scientologists and had 'pilloried' the FDA." But in the proceedings, Judge Gerhard Gesell reminded that insofar as Scientology was a legitimate religion, the government and the courts could not regulate the use of the E-meter. He noted that "as a matter of formal doctrine, the church professes to have abandoned any contention that there is a scientific basis for claiming cures resulting from E-meter use." Continued Gesell: "You can write about Scientology and dianetics until the cows come home—whether it is right or wrong—and the government could not regulate it."

Judge Gesell ruled that the E-meter could "be used or sold or distributed only for use in bona fide religious counseling." The device, he said, "should bear a prominent, clearly visible notice warning that any person using it for . . counseling of any kind is forbidden by law to represent that there is any medical or scientific basis for believing or asserting that the device is useful in the diagnosis, treatment, or prevention of any disease."

Willoughby felt the ruling put undue restrictions on Scientology and later wrote,

If the same rule were to be applied to certain artifacts of Christianity—holy water, prayer cloths, anointing oils, sacred images, icons—it is doubtful the courts would ever hear the end of the resulting litigation. Are the various claims to healing in the New Testament—widely disseminated over the air, via television, in books and

literature, and publicly advertised meetings—
ever going to be subjected to the same curbs?

It is unthinkable that someday the Scriptures
themselves might be labeled! Yet, is not the
principle, if not the scope, present in the court's
setting of limits on how the Church of Scientology may use its chief artifact?

He hadn't "flown the coop from Christianity to
Scientology. I haven't—not by a long shot," he
insisted. He understood "why certain psychiatrists
have initiated and carried out the war with Scientology . . . and how misinformation . . . printed
unquestioningly in the press can paint a real bad
picture of them." He knew "at least as many people
who have paid handsomely for psychiatric help as
. . . have paid just about as handsomely for help
from Scientology."

Arguments on the legality and usefulness of
Scientology aside, it must be said that it is an expensive religion. To keep advancing, a member
must pay and pay and pay. The sect is not likely
to enlist many poor people!

And for a religion that uses some of the terminology and symbols of Christianity, Scientology
has a strange code of ethics. Scientology "Scripture" includes such statements as "Never fear to
hurt another in a just cause."

Scientology, like many other cults, exalts its
founder as final authority. It deifies man and denies
sin. The word *man* is often capitalized in Scientology writings. Man does not need deliverance
from an outside, supreme God. He can climb out
of his troubles by following the upward path laid
down by Ron Hubbard. For a price.

Erhard Seminars Training (est) lays no claim to special treatment as a religion. It functions as an educational foundation. More to the point, it appears to be a money-making stewpot of ideas lifted from Eastern religions, Western behavioral science, and modern brainwashing.

Est seeks to rip from the mind all values implanted by parents, school, church, and larger society and to implant the idea that only what is experienced personally can be true and worthwhile. Self-satisfaction, self-fulfillment, and self-survival become the ultimate good. Everyone wills his own fate and if a friend or neighbor suffers, it is his own fault.

Erhard Seminar Training is named for the founding guru Werner Erhard, alias Jack Frost, alias Jack Rosenberg, who once sold used cars and trained book salesmen.

Born in a Philadelphia suburb, Rosenberg, according to *Newsweek,* graduated from high school, married, then seven years later "abandoned" his wife and three children, and "covered his tracks" by changing his name. Over the next several years, while working at various jobs, he experimented with several techniques of consciousness-raising from the smorgasbord of Eastern religions. Finally in 1971, while driving along a San Francisco highway, he received the "enlightenment" to which 83,000 people, including John Dean of Watergate fame, have each given $250 and 60 hours of time to share.

An est crash course is worse than a weekend boot camp. Assembled in a bare hotel ballroom, and presided over by Erhard or an approved top sergeant, trainees are not permitted to eat, drink, stretch, or go to the bathroom. During the "processes" (exercises) of giving up their "acts" (previous beliefs and values), some cry, faint, vomit, urinate on the floor, or collapse in physical exhaustion. They get no sympathy from the leader, who growls periodically, "You're just a tube! Tube! Tube! You're so hung up over what goes through you that you can't get on with getting it."

Getting what? A new inner "space" of the mind into which each can retreat from the world and alter consciousness at will. In this new experience of self-satisfaction the world is perfect, shame and guilt are no burden, truth is whatever you wish to believe, and suffering is the result of unrealized consciousness. Everything outside is illusion and has no meaning or purpose. Only your experience counts.

Here is the big hitch. The est experience is always in the present. Once realized, the experience becomes obsolete. One must go on to another experience and another and another, never able to rest at any fixed point. What one "gets," to use Erhard's term, is always formless, timeless, and valueless. Est, in sum, is Zen irrationality. One is getting and never getting, arriving and never arriving, pursuing the absurd in a race that goes on forever.

Est's guru is accused of manipulating troubled psyches for profit. The whole process, critics say, is simply a mechanical, Orwellian imitation of whatever Erhard wants trainees to do.

Moral philosopher Peter Marin has found Erhard's operation to be "in many ways the logical extension of the whole human potential movement of the past decade." Continued Marin in his

Harper's (October, 1975) article, "The New Narcissism":

> The refusal to consider moral complexities, the denial of history and a larger community, the disappearance of the Other, the exaggerations of the will, the reduction of all experience to a set of platitudes—all of that is to be found in embryonic form in almost all modern therapy.

The newer therapies, such as est, have gone one dangerous step further, Marin thinks. "Whereas the older therapies merely ignored moral and historical concerns, the new ones destroy or replace them. They become . . . a way of defining history and determining morality . . .

"The trend in therapy is toward the deification of the isolated self."

One result is that counselors now report a tidal wave of patients with narcissistic problems (infantile fascination with and admiration of oneself). Explained psychoanalyst Donald Kaplan in *Time*: "Other people exist like a candy machine. If there's no candy left, the narcissist starts kicking the machine."

Scientology, est, and other lesser-known consciousness-raising therapies proclaim a life-style that stands opposite Christ's formula for meaningful life fulfillment:

"For whosoever will save his life [in self-seeking] shall lose it: but whosoever will lose his life for My sake [in self-denying service to others] . . . shall save it" (Luke 9:24).

9

Mo's Storm Troopers

Somewhere in Europe or the Middle East a tall, thin-faced, fiftyish man with white hair and a trim little goatee is dictating a new revelation. Known to his followers as "Mo"—for Moses, he is also called David, Daniel, Aquarius, and God's Anointed. Of known Scandinavian descent, he claims kinship with Robert E. Lee, Theodore Roosevelt, Willy Brandt, John Charles Thomas, and Humphrey Bogart. And he has also bragged of being filled with the Holy Spirit from the time he was born.

Mo's newest revelation will be processed in a "print pantry" and mailed in three versions. The uncensored "strong meat" version—perhaps containing vulgarities, erotic visions, and hard-to-believe prophecies—will go to elders, shepherds, and leaders of tribes. A censored draft will be sent to disciples, and a third, the most bland, will be mailed to babes who are on a "milk" diet. This third variant will be printed in greatest quantity for hawking for donations on the streets of the free world's great cities.

Moses Berg is the strange leader of the Children of God (COG), the best known of several cultic spin-offs from the Jesus Revolution which flowered in the late 1960s and early '70s. Praised in the beginning by mainstream evangelical church leaders, the Children are now regarded as misguided, dangerous fanatics.

Berg himself, whom the Children believe to be the Prophet of the end times and leader of the True Remnant, is regarded by some nonadmirers as a psychotic paranoid suffering from delusions of grandeur, and a dirty old man with a history of perversion extending back to childhood.

In understanding how the Children arose, developed, and were led into strange paths by Berg, we must begin with the movement from which they sprang.

The Jesus Revolution was never planned. It flared from a spontaneous combustion among young people disillusioned with the "rags" of war, politics, drugs, free sex, and religious trips that had not satisfied. First noticed in 1967 in the hippie Haight-Ashbury district in San Francisco and along decadent Sunset Strip in Los Angeles, it spread rapidly to other cities, carried by hitchhiking Jesus Freaks and underground newspapers. There was never any overarching structure or systematic theology; only a unity of heartbeat as thousands of youth turned on to Jesus and began showing His love.

It quickly became a media event. *Time,* in an upbeat, glowing 12-page cover story, stated, "There is a morning freshness to it all, a buoyant atmosphere of hope and love along with the usual rebel zeal."

Most elders felt positive vibrations. Cynics conceded that the Jesus trip had to be better than the drug trip. Fired-up church leaders hoped it would bring revival and moral cleansing to the whole country. Astute observers saw one big danger: inadequately trained leadership.

The fear was well-founded. The earliest leaders arose from the ranks. But once the movement became publicized, older "pastors" began corralling young sheep. There was no board of reference to check them out. Some, such as Southern Baptist evangelist Arthur Blessit, were mature and pure of motive. Others were less desirable.

In 1968 David Brandt Berg, then 49, began managing a coffeehouse in Huntington Beach, California for the nationwide Teen Challenge ministry. He appeared to have good credentials for the job. He had worked since 1954 as a public relations man for TV evangelist Fred Jordan. Before that he had been a Christian and Missionary Alliance pastor in Arizona and a youth evangelist. His parents had also been evangelists and his mother had some fame as a prophetess.

It was not then known that Berg had had a troubled childhood. Later he would brag to COG elders of sexual virility before 10 and of hearing strange voices when he sat alone in a tree. It would also come out that he had been ejected from the Alliance denomination.

In Huntington Beach the coffeehouse was at the center of the Jesus Revolution in southern California. The fields were ripe and in no time Berg had young disciples "fishing" on beaches, around schools, and in church youth groups for additions to the "Teens for Christ" organization he had formed.

They were also called "Revolutionaries for Christ," a more fitting title. Their strategy was to surround a young stranger with assurances of love and care, insert his name in appropriate Scripture verses and hymns, then implore him to go back on the bus with them to the coffeehouse.

Once he had made a commitment, they challenged the new convert to drop all ties with straight society (job, school, family) and join God's "army" full time. For this they cited Jesus' call to Peter and Andrew, "Follow Me, and I will make you fishers of men. And they straightway left their nets, and followed Him" (Matt. 4:19-20). And the example of the first church at Jerusalem: "And all that believed were together, and had all things common; and sold their possessions and goods, and parted them to all men, as every man had need" (Acts 2:44-45).

Communal living was then the "in thing" among Jesus people, making the appeal to join a "full-time" missionary ministry even stronger.

At first local churches welcomed Berg's "Revolutionaries," inviting them in to give testimonies. But when church youth began joining up, doors closed. Whereupon Berg turned a new trick and organized a "raiding party."

Some 50 strong, the "Revolutionaries" would arrive at a targeted church about 11:30 A.M., when the pastor was starting his sermon. Pushing aside shocked ushers, they would tromp down carpeted aisles and sprawl on the floor before the pulpit. There, in plain view of everyone, they would shout loud amens and Hallelujahs each time the preacher said something they liked.

One Sunday they spoiled communion for an Episcopal church, wailing, singing, and jabbering in gibberish during the most solemn moments. The disturbance made the front page of a newspaper. Berg was elated and invited the reporter to join them for the next raid at the futuristic Garden Grove Community Church. They were bodily thrown out and got an even bigger story.

Weekdays they blitzed schools. When police dragged them off a junior college campus, they donned sandwich signs and paraded along sidewalks outside.

Reveling in the notoriety, Berg announced a prophecy from his ailing mother: California was going to be hit with a horrendous earthquake and drop into the sea. Earthquake predictions were nothing new, but coming from the colorful leader of the "Revolutionaries," this one made headlines.

Exuberant over getting the attention he felt he had so long deserved, Berg led a convoy of vans and old buses to San Francisco. There they stormed into posh Grace Cathedral, shouting, "Repent! Repent!" Moving on to nearby San Rafael, they created so much havoc that the town council took up a collection to pay expenses to get them out of town.

When Berg received an invitation from an old pastor friend, Ted Ware, to come to Tucson and start a teen center, he ordered his flock to pack. His excuse was that California was going to be destroyed in the earthquake predicted by his mother. He had already broken with the Teen Challenge ministry, and perhaps realized his "Revolutionaries" had exhausted whatever good will they had earlier built up in California.

Berg and his "Revolutionaries" blew into Tucson like a whirlwind, denouncing local churches and denominations as "abominations," disrupting services as they had done in California, and splitting Ware's congregation into two camps.

Ironically, it was their practice of helping runaways that ruined the scene for them in Tucson. A boy who had been severely beaten by his father came to them for shelter. They turned him over to juvenile authorities, who gave him back to his brutal parent. The boy committed suicide. The "Revolutionaries" got the blame. After a second runaway killed himself, Berg pulled out with his family and a church secretary, Maria, for Texas, leaving son-in-law John Treadwell in charge of the "Revolutionaries."

When Treadwell helped a young girl in trouble with the law to escape, the police came after him. He and the others jumped in vans and raced at top speed for the New Mexico border. By the time they got to Fort Worth, Texas, Berg and his family and Maria had moved on to Canada.

Another minister friend of Berg's let the Treadwell group stay at his church's camp. Treadwell was more moderate than Berg and tried a new tack. At his request the boys cut their hair short and the girls wore clean, long granny dresses. They were respectful when visiting churches and asking for donations to help poor people and youths on drugs. Having heard nothing but good of the Jesus Movement, Fort Worthers opened their churches and their hearts. Pastors praised them. The group increased rapidly.

Berg treated his son-in-law's success as betrayal. He called long distance to straighten him out, then sent his wife, Jane, and son, Paul, to follow up.

Their arrival provoked a fierce argument. While they were debating, Berg called to announce a new prophecy. A "great confusion" would soon come on America and the country would fall. Treadwell was to close down his operations and bring everyone to a meeting in northern Illinois.

Treadwell didn't want to leave, but Berg had ordered submission. As they were packing, Berg telephoned another order. All elders—those who had been with the group six months or longer—must "choose" wives immediately.

Andy Hall (assumed last name), in charge of soliciting provisions, was one who hesitated. He had joined the group at Huntington Beach. Now in his early 20s, he was old enough to be married. But he just couldn't see picking out one of the girls like a piece of merchandise.

"If you can't decide," Treadwell said, "I'll have to find the one God has for you."

Treadwell later announced, "The Lord has given you Susan."

Susan, a classic redhead, had joined the group not long after Andy. But except for going on witnessing teams together they hardly knew one another.

"Go ask her," Treadwell pressed.

Andy wanted to do God's will. It had been drilled into him that he was to submit to spiritual authority. Still he was too embarrassed to propose directly. Finally Treadwell said, "I'll put my instructions on a tape. Play that to her."

Andy took the tape and asked her to listen.

When it stopped, he blushingly asked, "Well, what do you think?"

Her face matched her hair. "I don't know what to say. It's something, I guess, to pray about." Then she ran crying to the girls' quarters.

She got no sympathy there. One girl said bluntly, "You're just rebelling against God's will."

At prayer meeting the next evening, another girl gave a prophecy: "God has given you, Andy, this handmaiden, Susan, to be your wife. Take her and fear not." Prophecies related to the pairing of other couples followed.

Andy took Susan outside to talk. "I want to wait," she pleaded.

"I'm not ready either," he agreed.

They went back and told the others. "No, no, no!" their friends cried.

Suddenly the girl who had given the first prophecy shouted, "God says, 'If thou will not be married this very night, I will utterly smite you.' Thus saith the Lord."

Andy and Susan succumbed to group pressure and did what they felt God wanted them to do. They had an awkward conjugal night.

Shortly after the new "marriages" (legalities were taken care of later) were consummated, the Fort Worth group started north. They met the Bergs and others in Illinois State Park on the cold shore of Lake Michigan, north of Chicago. Here in late November 1969, Berg divided them into 12 tribes and gave everyone Bible names.

Berg became "Moses," his wife, Jane, "Mother Eve." Oddly, he named his son-in-law, John Treadwell, "Jethro," who was the father-in-law of Moses in the Bible. Treadwell's wife, Linda, became

"Deborah," or "Queen Debby," as the group called her. Faith Berg Dietrich, another Berg daughter, was allowed to keep her own first name. Her husband Arnie was christened "Joshua" or "Big Josh." Berg's bachelor sons, Paul and Jonathan, were named "Aaron" and "Hosea" respectively. Andy Hall, the reluctant bridegroom, became "Hezekiah."

Clad in red sackcloth (burlap begged from factories) and with ashes daubed on their faces, the "Revolutionaries" set out in their buses and vans to warn the nation of its impending fall. During the next few months they appeared like specters from ancient Israel on television screens. One group held a vigil at the trial of the "Chicago Seven" antiwar protesters. Another bunch paraded somberly before cameras at the Texas-Arkansas football game. Another busload traveled to Washington and trooped by the casket of Senator Everett Dirksen lying in state in the Capitol rotunda.

Always stone-faced, they walked single file, clanking their staves and chanting, "Woe, woe, woe, woe!" If Berg's motive was to gain publicity, he succeeded beyond his wildest dream.

Berg grabbed hungrily at newspaper stories. When a reporter described them as "children of God," Berg declared, "That's our name. From now on we are the Children of God." For Berg it all fit into place. He was the one God had appointed to lead his chosen children out of "Egypt" (the United States) to the "Promised Land" of a soon-to-come millennial kingdom.

Berg announced that the final countdown of the last years of world history would begin in 1985, climaxed by the Second Coming of Christ in 1993, "when there will be millions of us." When someone noted Christ had said no one could know the day or hour of His return, Berg countered, "Yeah, but He didn't say we couldn't know the year."

But Berg was not ready to leave "Egypt" yet. More "children" had to be enlisted and trained. He struck a deal with his old employer Fred Jordan. The TV evangelist would provide the Children training bases at his ranches in California and Texas, a tax shelter for contributors, and ministerial draft protection for the young men. For their part, the Children would keep up the ranches and appear on Jordan's TV program to show viewers that he was winning young people, thus helping to bring in more donations.

Jordan would later claim investing heavily in the Children, spending $98,000 for transportation and operating expenses, $500,000 in promotion, and even providing "Mo" Berg a $1,000 monthly salary.

The Children were already mysteriously intriguing to the American public. The linkup with Jordan gave them respectability. Media people competed for stories. The biggest puff was an NBC-TV news special in January 1971. Hundreds of youth wrote or called network stations afterward, asking information on how to join. One boy drove across Texas looking for Jordan's ranch, a sign on his car asking, "CHILDREN OF GOD, WHERE ARE YOU?"

Some leaders of the Jesus Movement, previously suspicious of Berg, now eyed him with admiration. He had organization and discipline while other segments of the movement were fragmenting. Three big stars brought large flocks into Berg's fold: Linda Meissner of Seattle, Russell Gribbs of Vancouver, and David Hoyt of San Francisco. Meissner's decision broke up her marriage. Hoyt's action resulted in an evangelical publisher (Zondervan) canceling a book he had been writing about false cults. Across the country, other leaders of the Jesus Movement looked on with dismay.

The favorable publicity followed by the new influx pushed the Children to a probable 3,000, certainly no more than 5,000. This proved to be their high water mark. After the summer of 1971 they began shrinking as troubles assailed them.

Many of the arranged marriages were in trouble. At Fred Jordan's Texas ranch, elders complained their wives wouldn't submit. Berg, now living on a hill dubbed "Mt. Sinai," called a colony meeting and ordered the wives to get in line. "I have a list of the disobedient," he threatened. "If you don't do it with your husbands," he reportedly said, "I'll do it to you right in front of everybody." His bluntness, accompanied by vulgar language, shocked disciples and babes who were uninformed about his growing preoccupation with sexual matters.

A broken-hearted Mother Eve had told the inner circle of elders about her husband's latest revelation. God had told him, he claimed, to take Maria as a wife. She represented the new church bride of Christ, while Eve symbolized the old church which God had rejected. But Eve could sleep with him every other night.

Then the elders heard their leader had taken still another concubine, and had fathered a baby by her. Jethro Treadwell was very upset and tried to find some justification in Scripture for his father-in-law's behavior. The best conclusion he could reach was that the Scripture which says an elder should be the husband of one wife meant *at least* one wife.

Despite the elders' pledge to secrecy, word of Berg's troubled marital affairs leaked out. Grumblings increased. There was whispered talk of mutiny.

Everyone had signed the "revolutionary sheet," giving themselves and all earthly possessions to the group. But there was always the possibility of Satan luring immature believers away.

Guards were stationed around the premises—"to keep angry parents and other enemies from kidnapping babes, and infiltrators from planting narcotics that would invite police raids," rank and file were told. Incoming mail was censored because Satan would offer any bribe—dope, money, a plane trip to Europe—to get young missionaries out of God's service. Outgoing mail was read and phone calls monitored to discover "spiritual needs" in the family.

The "two by two" rule was strictly enforced. No one went anywhere without a companion. Not for a walk. Not even to the bathroom. Always someone was there quoting Scripture to ward off suggestions of Satan.

All day and into the night members obediently recited Bible verses. Loudspeakers blared out selected Scriptures and quotations from Moses Berg. After lights out, tape recorders ran in bedrooms, keeping up the pressure.

The Children at the Texas and California ranches and at other locations were constantly being reminded that they were the chosen remnant and on the right path while "Egypt"—the satanic system of government, corporations, labor unions, churches, opposing parents—was doomed to destruction. But it was all right to secure provisions for the wilderness journey from the world, even by deceit, if necessary. That was "spoiling Egypt," as the Children of Israel had done when taking jewelry from their former slave-masters. And businessmen could be approached for donations, because they were like the pagan "kings" who had helped the Israelites.

Still there was a leakage of members. When someone announced, "I can't take it any longer; I'm leaving," a circle would form around him chanting Bible warnings and predicting accidents, disease, and other terrible calamities for "running away from God." The result was that those who did leave sneaked past the guards in the middle of the night and walked to the highway to hitch rides.

The Children were also constantly told that they were under God's special protection. But accidents such as the death of the field boss, Abner, in a motorcycle race with Jethro, were hard to explain.

Visiting parents were another big problem. When a parent showed up at the gate, the guard announced a "ten-thirty-sixer." The number stood for Matthew 10:36, a verse which every member had memorized: "And a man's foes shall be they of his own household."

Another code word was "Selah," a term used in the Psalms to indicate a pause in worship, but which meant to the Children, "Button your lips. Don't spill any secrets." With so many strangers from other COG colonies coming to the world training headquarters in Texas, members had to know which visitors could be trusted.

The biblical names came in handy when worried parents came looking for their children. When a couple inquired for, say, a daughter named Ann

Jordan, the members could say they didn't know anyone by that name. And, in truth, many didn't know the real names of other members.

The winds of publicity turned cold. An eviction notice came from Fred Jordan. He cited only "disobedience" of spiritual authority and doctrinal errors. But he must also have realized that the controversial Children and their unpredictable leader had become more a liability than an asset to his television solicitations.

About the same time the Children were hit hard from another direction when aggrieved parents got together and formed "Free Our Children from the Children of God" (FREECOG). The sparkplug of the group was William Rambur, a retired naval officer from San Diego, who charged that his daughter, a nurse, had been "brainwashed" by the group and was "not herself."

Other parents joined Rambur and his wife in a demonstration against the Children in front of the Federal Building in Dallas. Mr. and Mrs. John Moody were from New York. Their daughter Melissa had joined COG while a student at the University of Texas in Austin. They had brought her home once to talk with their minister, Norman Vincent Peale, only to lose her again. When Mrs. Moody had gone to the ranch, the elders had made her wait almost an hour while Melissa, renamed Patience, was "revved up" to resist parental appeal.

The Dallas demonstration brought a $1.1 million suit for libel and slander against the FREECOG parents. The Children also announced that about 30 parents had organized THANK COG to show their support of the group.

THANK COG soon folded while FREECOG

informally teamed up with deprogrammer Ted Patrick, then a community relations consultant to
California's Governor Reagan. During the next two
years, Patrick helped FREECOG parents "rescue"
and "rehabilitate" over 100 COG "victims."

Ejected from Jordan's ranches and under fire
from coast to coast, the Children began dispers-
ing abroad. Some followed Berg to Europe, where
his son Paul died in a mysterious accident. Some
took flights to New Zealand and Australia. Some
filtered into Mexico and Central America. Those
who remained in the U.S. were scattered in small
colonies.

Their record in the U.S. was repeated in other
countries. First they were received by parents and
church leaders as legitimate members of the Jesus
Movement. Then as their methods and beliefs
became known, disillusionment set in and they were
labeled "dangerous."

A chastened English Baptist pastor wrote, "Having backed this movement (COG) more than any
since they arrived in Britain, I repent for having
encouraged . . . false teaching, dishonoring to
Christ."

Elsewhere there were more setbacks. David Hoyt,
who had led scores of Jesus People into COG,
departed, confessing sorrowfully that he had been
deceived. His wife stayed behind.

In Guatemala, Andy Hall, the "provisioner" for
the defunct Texas operation, and his wife Susan
sought counsel from evangelical missionaries. They
and their three small children were helped to return
home. But they were not free of the damage
wrought by COG. After marital counseling, they
agreed on a trial separation. While apart from

Andy, Susan was visited by loyal COG members and persuaded to return. She took a new Bible name and refused to let her husband see his children. Recently, however, she came back to her husband.

The sledgehammer blow on COG's dwindling U.S. force fell in October 1974, when New York Attorney General Louis J. Lefkowitz released a devastating 65-page investigative report charging COG's leaders with mentally and sexually abusing young converts. The report was based on interviews with 75 witnesses—present and former COG members, parents, and others having special knowledge of the group.

Item: The organizational structure of COG was a pyramid, descending from Berg, through his wife, four children and spouses, and below them in descending order, elders, colony leaders, tribe leaders, assistant tribe leaders, disciples, and babes.

Item: Attempts to inquire into the finances of the central organization had met with "defiance." Financial records had been taken from Texas out of the country. "The obvious inference from the testimony of ex-COGs and parents is that monies are directed to the key leaders for their personal use and enjoyment. Funds came from sale of new members' possessions, from parents, local merchants, sale of public Mo Letters, and from wealthy individuals (one had contributed $75,000)."

Item: Members had been directed to "subvert" legal processes. Quoting from a Mo Letter on "Publications" for leaders:

You can ask to see the warrant—make sure who it's for, and while you are stalling, someone else can inform the disciple involved, who then has a perfect right to run out of the back door if he wants to.

Item: Members had been taught to reject their parents. From a Mo Letter: "You, my dear parents are the greatest rebels against God. . . . To hell with your devilish system. . . . God is going to destroy you and save us."

Item: Members had been told all government was evil. "It's time for the rape of America. . . . She doesn't deserve respect: She's an old whore!"

Item: Education had been termed by Berg, "another part of the whore's sorcery . . . to keep the fornication going." The *Report* cited students dropping out of school to join COG, for example, a medical student convinced by elders that only God could heal.

Item: Members had been indoctrinated with the assistance of mental and physical fatigue and intense memorization of selected Bible verses taken out of context, climaxed by introduction to Mo letters and COG lesson plans which supplanted the Bible as the main source of instruction. COG leaders were guilty of "tampering with the personalities of converts . . . to change established behavior patterns."

Item: The leadership demanded instant obedience. An ex-member said this extended even to killing.

Item: A 14-year-old testified of having been raped repeatedly in a COG colony. When she objected, a leader told her such forced sex would "increase the tribe." Sarah Berg, Moses' former daughter-in-law, testified that Berg had forced her to have intercourse with his son—in his presence—a number of times before they were married. After her first child was born, Berg had requested her to submit to him sexually.

The *Report* also cited excerpts from Mo letters justifying incest on the basis that Adam and Eve's sons must have married their sisters, and mentioning that he (Berg) had had his first "intercourse at the early age of seven."

Item: After Sarah Berg's divorce in 1973 and her husband's subsequent mysterious death, she had tried to locate her young son. COG denied knowing of his whereabouts, but testimony from witnesses indicated that the child was in the care of a COG member in British Columbia.

The report concluded that "despite the shocking facts outlined, no direct action" could be undertaken because of "the constitutional protection of the First Amendment." It was hoped that "publication of this report would awaken the public."

In its response to the N.Y. Attorney General's *Report*, COG ignored most of the specific charges, claiming misrepresentation and vilification by witnesses, and saying that such persecution was only proof the Children were the true followers of Jesus. Most of COG's reply was given to critical press reports on Ted Patrick's deprogramming of youth belonging to more straight religious groups.

The New York investigation was widely reported in world media. Since then COG has gone deeper underground in the U.S., though members still sell Mo letters in major cities and solicit donations. Like some other cultists, the Children often use the names of fronts and even respectable organizations in making their pitches.

They are more obvious abroad. In NATO countries, where American forces are stationed, COG members are befriending lonely American soldiers. In predominantly Catholic countries such as Spain and Portugal, they are sweet-talking Catholic prelates—a dramatic switch since 1969 when members draped a casket in black and disrupted a high mass in a Catholic church in Quebec.

Berg spelled out his Catholic strategy in a letter to lieutenants:

"We are now beginning to invade the Catholic countries of the world and we are going to have to be pro-Catholic. . . . They believe much the same as we do! They also believe in communes, in forsaking all, in brainwashing and memorization! . . . Go partake of their little Eucharist, go kneel with them in their chapels. . . . They don't know anything else. . . . Play along with them. . . . Join the circus."

Taking another turn, Berg is cozying up to Col. Muammar Quaddafi, the quixotic Libyan dictator. A widely distributed COG phamphlet portrays "Miss Europe" in a bridal gown nestling up to the Arab strongman with "parents"—U.S.A. and U.S.S.R.—frowning from the background and an approving God gazing down from above.

Berg's obsession with sex appears to have deepened. Some letters border on the pornographic and blasphemous. One compares sexual delight with the spiritual wonders of "total intimacy with a very sexy, naked God Himself in a wild orgy of the Spirit." Another title "Hooker for Jesus," pictures a nubile mermaid impaled on a hook making advances to a nude youth, and calls on female colony members to be "little flirty fishes" for Jesus. The idea is that girls should use sex as "bait" to attract new converts.

What Berg and his COG remnant will do next is unpredictable since they have placed themselves above convention, society, government, and commonly accepted ethics of the Bible.

10

A Bottomless Barrel

Moses Berg's Children of God is the most prominent in the jumble of new cults flying under the
banner of Christianity. Hundreds of other deviant
groups the world over, scores in the United States,
are headed by guru-type teachers who, like Berg,
claim to have discovered truth which mainstream
Christianity has missed during the past 19 centuries.

These groups tend to be tightly knit, militantly
missionary, and wary of reporters. They flourish in
a free society under the protection of freedom of
religion. In this same free society, those who disagree with them have the right to publish information about them.

We can consider only a few of the more aggressive cultic "Christian" heresies. Much of our
information is sketchy simply because little is
presently known about these groups. Some are
obviously heretical. Others sincerely see themselves
in a prophetic role, called to lead the main body

of Christians out of error and into truth as they know it.

The Church of Armageddon This bizarre cult professes dedication "to the creation of one pure, beautiful, and holy community where men are free to live in accordance with God's way—the way shown to us in the New Testament of Jesus Christ." But Brooks P. Russell, Chief Criminal Investigator for King County (Seattle), Washington, where the cult is domiciled, calls the Armageddon commune "a danger to our society . . . so careful to operate barely within the law that criminal justice agencies are effectively barred from taking any action against them."

The founder and present spiritual authority is Paul Erdman, alias Love Israel. He has a record of 12 arrests with the Seattle police department for offenses that include drunkenness, robbery, embezzlement, and reckless driving. He declines press interviews and speaks only through three elders.

Erdman, according to Chief Investigator Russell, lives in a Swiss chalet-style home, furnished with Persian rugs, silver, and crystal. Other more modest residences nearby are occupied by about 75 church members. Erdman has a wife, children, and a beautiful teenage maid.

An initiate exchanges his family surname for "Israel" and takes as his first name some virtue which the family believes it needs, such as Strength, Serious, Charity, or Trust. His new date of birth is his day of acceptance into the church.

All members share a common mailing address which, according to Russell, "makes it convenient for Love and the elders to censure or withhold the members' correspondence." Each surrenders all his money and personal property rights to Love Israel, who holds and disburses funds for the group.

At the wish of Love Israel, members may be "bonded" in marriage or "unbonded" in divorce. It is rumored that Love Israel tries out a new bride before bonding her to a husband.

Female members are expected to serve males and give birth to children, who will be cared for communally. "Mother" is an abominable word in the group. When asked if a certain child was hers, one young woman replied, "He came from this temple, but he belongs to the Family." The women do not eat until the men are served and then they are permitted only one-third portions. One woman who defected said she had been forbidden to speak unless spoken to.

Radio, television, newspapers, books, clocks and calendars are forbidden to the membership, even when they travel to work in the fruit harvest in eastern Washington. Only Love Israel and four elders may operate vehicles.

A statement of faith and practice was issued following the death of two members. Solidity and Reverence Israel had died from inhaling an industrial chemical in a plastic bag. "God is stronger than any chemical," an elder said and cited the classic text of Appalachian snake handlers, Mark 16:18. He explained that those who breathed "tell-u-all [toluene] with unselfish motives received positive experiences," while those who breathed "greedily experienced negative effects."

Members meditate while staring at a blank wall. They eat meals "as the body and blood of our Lord Jesus Christ, in daily celebration of the Lord's Supper." To prove their faith, they participate in a "shock" contest. Members sit in a circle and hold hands, with one person holding metal connected to an electrical outlet. A switch is thrown, sending the current around the circle. The last one still holding on to the connection proves his faith.

Case history: Kathy Crampton, a former Girl Scout leader in Redondo Beach, California, was the "last person" friends "ever expected to get messed up with a cult." But shortly after breaking up with her boyfriend and spending Christmas holidays at home, she returned to college in Washington and was drawn into the Armageddon Church.

"Dear Mom and Dad," she wrote in a first letter. "I'm living in a good Christian home where they read the Bible a lot. Love, Kathy."

Her next letter began only, "Hello," and stated she had a new family and wouldn't be writing home anymore.

Her parents' hurried reply came back stamped RETURN TO SENDER—ADDRESSEE UNKNOWN with a poem:
Eye to eye
Hand to hand
We'd love to see you
In our land.

Alarmed and upset, Mrs. Crampton went to Seattle and demanded to see Kathy. When Kathy was brought out, her mother noticed that one side of her face was scabby and infected and her personality had drastically changed. "My name is now Corinth," she said numbly. "I am 89 years old and in heaven, where I will never die." She refused medical aid.

Mrs. Crampton begged public and private agencies for help in getting Kathy out. Because Kathy was 19 and an adult, the agencies said, nothing could be done.

Desperate, the Cramptons turned to controversial deprogrammer Ted Patrick for help. Patrick permitted a CBS-TV camera crew to do an on-scene documentary of Kathy's "abduction" and trip back to San Diego for deprogramming. When her parents thought she was on the road to recovery, they allowed her to attend a beach party. There she bolted from her escort, ran to the highway, and hitched a ride. The CBS crew, still pursuing the story, found her several days later back in the group and living under a new name, Dedication.

The Way International The Way resents being called a cult. The founder has respectable, establishment, ministerial training and credentials. The group asserts belief in God, the Bible, Jesus Christ, salvation, an abundant Christian life, and eternal life in a personal, bodily existence. But we shall see that The Way is not just another evangelical denomination or parachurch ministry to youth.

Founder-leader Victor Paul Wierwille graduated from Mission House College, a United Church of Christ school in Wisconsin, and earned the master's degree in practical theology from Princeton Seminary. He also claims to have studied at the University of Chicago Divinity School and Moody Bible Institute, and to have received a doctorate from Pike's Peak Theological Seminary. The latter school is unaccredited.

Wierwille was frustrated at the "shallowness" of the ministry after two years in the pastorate. Denominations didn't "care about teaching God's Word. They perpetuate themselves . . . put people in straight jackets, atrophy their lives." He was ready to "let God have the whole thing, unless there were real genuine answers that I wouldn't ever have to back up on. That's when He spoke to me audibly . . . He said He would teach me the Word as it has not been known since the first century if I would teach it to others."

He had doubts the next day and asked God to "give me a sign . . . let me see snow." When he closed his eyes the sky was clear. When he opened them, the snow was so thick, he "couldn't see the tanks of a filling station on the corner 75 feet away."

Wierwille purports to have discovered certain apostolic teaching "lost" to Christendom since the first century:

God is a duality, Father and Holy Spirit, and not a Trinity. Jesus Christ was "fathered" by God only to the extent that His life principle (soul) was miraculously inseminated into the woman who bore His body.

Jesus was perfect because His Father gave Him dominant "sinless" genes. But to worship Him as God is to violate the commandment, "Thou shalt have no other gods . . ." Jesus is merely the highest form of human existence.

Wierwille's "new Truth" is just another old heresy. The Monarchians, Ebionites, and Arians all denied the deity of Jesus during the era of the Church Fathers. Their teachings were condemned in church councils. Today Jehovah's Witnesses also maintain that Jesus is not God, though their interpretation of His existence differs from Wierwille's.

Wierwille also teaches there are two holy spirits. One is God. The other and lesser holy spirit (never in caps) was the "divinity within" lost through

Adam's fall. Hope was restored by Second Adam (Jesus), who because of perfect obedience, was exalted to a position from where He can restore the "gift of holy spirit" to salvation seekers. By receiving this spirit, which is separate from body and soul, believers find the secret of "abundant living."

The Way did not begin to grow rapidly until Wierwille instituted a "tree structure" in 1971. The headquarters in New Knoxville, Ohio, on the founder's old family homestead, is "The Roots." State units are "limbs"; city units, "branches"; and small Way Homes, "twig fellowships."

The Way now has several hundred Word-over-the-World Ambassadors (WOWS) signing up new students for Wierwille's "Abundant Life" correspondence course (cost $84). WOWS stay in line by attending regular—often daily—twig meetings where they listen to Wierwille's latest tapes and receive in-service training.

Way Corpsmen make a two-year commitment to work without salary at the farm headquarters. They help at the International Biblical Research Center, do farm chores, staff the correspondence school, prepare filmstrips, and man the printing and publishing operations. The Way publishes a newsletter, a magazine, and Wierwille's books.

A day at "The Roots" begins at 5:30 A.M. with exercise and a one-to-four mile run with Wierwille. After breakfast the corpsmen put in a full day's work, then fan out to nearby towns to "witness" during early evening hours.

Corpsmen are trained at The Way College in Emporia, Kansas. Formerly the College of Emporia, the campus was purchased for a bargain price from the United Presbyterian Church in 1974. The Presbyterian inscription "FOUNDED IN 1892" is reportedly still there, giving the impression that The Way wishes to build on the good will built up by the Presbyterians.

WOWS, corpsmen, students, and other members are expected to work vigorously, witness zealously, think positively, and show "Christian etiquette" to every person encountered. *Christianity Today,* in a five-paragraph report (December 20, 1974), said Wierwille held an "honorary doctorate" from "a reputed degree mill." The managing editor of *The Way* replied that the degree was "perfectly legitimate . . . not even 'honorary.'" He said the "corps of Way workers," as *Christianity Today* described them, should be called "the Way Corps." And he objected most strenuously to the inference in the title of the article, "Way Out in Kansas."

"If we are such a 'way-out' group," he demanded, "why don't you prove us wrong by rightly dividing God's Word instead of telling us how many theologies we contradict? . . . If you're ever honest with God's Word, you'll have to say Jesus Christ is not God."

The Way is even more unhappy about complaints from ex-members such as Suzanne Toler of Wichita Falls, Texas. In a statement filed for the 1976 Day of Affirmation and Protest in Washington, D.C., Miss Toler recalled:

Due to my participation in this cult, my personality changed completely. I lost my identity and was only what the cult wanted me to be—a smiling puppet. They taught me that God's work comes first, regardless of tests or school work. They made me feel guilty if I did not attend fellowship. My (nursing school) grades dropped from Bs to failing marks, which was not representative of my previous academic achievement.

Constant pressure was placed on members to become more committed to The Way ministry, making one feel that his commitment is to God, thus being a more binding agreement. Tremendous pressure was placed on members to keep them from questioning the ministry or dropping out of the group. One reaches the point that he believes in the integrity of the leader, Dr. Wierwille, and is no longer able to question his teachings. He destroys the individual's confidence . . . to interpret the Bible with the guidance of the Holy Spirit.

I realize that I was definitely brainwashed by subtle indoctrination techniques.

Opposition has not cooled the zeal of The Way and its founder. Though Wierwille did not reach his goal of having a twig fellowship in every U.S. community by the end of 1976, his cult is multiplying. About 2,000 new students reportedly sign up for the "Abundant Living" course each month.

The Local Church While researching for this book, I went to the modernistic, landscaped, Anaheim, California headquarters of The Local Church as a journalist and received the classic cold shoulder. The stocky man in the business office frowned and said, "We know of no prophet that has arisen from the press." My offer to buy books (clearly visible in a display case) by the founder-leader were refused. The representative would only say, "I found the truth here."

No religious group can expect to keep its teachings and operations secret for long in an open society. Inevitably, defectors will deliver training materials into the hands of critical outsiders, who will judge the group by its norms and beliefs. To the consternation of The Local Church, this is now happening, though not enough is known to give the analysis deserved.

The founder-leader is Witness Lee, a breakaway disciple from now deceased (1972) Watchman Nee. Nee founded local churches in China from the 1920s to the 1960s. His books on discipleship are still popular among American evangelicals, though some question his teaching that members should blindly submit to delegated authority in the church.

Witness Lee established "Local Churches" in Hong Kong and Taiwan before coming to southern California in 1969. Today the bellwether Local Church is in Anaheim, with others in major cities. When Lee is not traveling "among the brethren," he teaches at the Anaheim Church, which is housed in the same building with printing and publishing operations for all the scattered congregations. Little else is known about his life.

As is typical of cults, the Local Church claims to be the true expression of God's work on earth. Lee, like Victor Paul Wierwille, believes that key doctrinal truth has been lost since the first century and was only rediscovered by himself.

"Until there is a Local Church [his brand] in your locality," he writes, "you can never have the proper expression of the Body. . . . Do not try to be neutral . . . (or) try to reconcile the denominations with the Local Church. You can never reconcile them. . . . The only way to follow the Lord absolutely is to go the way of the Local Church."

Robert L. Passantino, Research Associate of the Christian Research Institute, and his wife, have "researched over 500 hours" on the Local Church and are convinced it teaches wrong doctrines about God, the Church, man, and salvation.

The Passantinos call the Local Church's doctrine of God "modalistic monarchianism" a heresy rejected by church councils in the third century. "The modalist (One Person in three modes or manifestations) describes God as one Nature and one individual Person who projects Himself in three distinct modes or aspects of His Being." The biblical Trinity, according to Dr. Walter R. Martin, Director of the CRI, is "three eternally distinct persons: the Father, the Son, and the Holy Spirit . . . within the nature of the one true God."

Lee holds three basic errors about the Church, say the Passantinos: (1) it (The Local Church) "becomes God manifest in the flesh," (2) The Local Church "is the only representative of the body of Christ on earth," (3) "there is to be only one unified gathering of believers in any one city or 'locality.'"

The Local Church also teaches, they add, "that fallen man is 'mingled' with Satan, and Satan and he become inseparable. To be saved all he "has to do is say 'O Lord Jesus' three times and even if he has no intention of believing, he will still be saved." Regenerated or saved man is "mingled" with the Holy Spirit so that "now it is possible for man to have more than a created, human spirit."

In worship, The Local Church "pray-reads" the Bible aloud, punctuating phrases with "amen," "hallelujah,' and "O Lord Jesus Christ," voices ris-

ing and falling in programmed unison. Scriptures
are divided into single and double word groups and
rearranged so as to obscure the meaning. This is
the "best way to have our spirits released," Witness
Lee says, "because pray-reading the Word exercises our spirit and does not give us time to use our
mind." Eastern mysticism uses somewhat the same
method in chanting a mantra to eliminate conscious
thought and alter the consciousness.

Witness Lee says the "all-inclusive Christ" is
both "the Creator and the creation." He sees man
and God coming together in a unity of essence as
water and tea diffuse to become one beverage. The
individual's identity, feelings, and intellect are
swallowed up in the cosmic Christ. Again, this is
parallel to the Eastern concept of dissolving individual consciousness into the all-inclusive Absolute.
In either case the result is mindlessness given over
to the control of an authoritative teacher.

The Local Church seems to appeal more to mid-
dle-age, middle-class white adults than to young
people and minorities. Most members come from
mainline Protestant denominations and Plymouth
Brethren assemblies. A typical member was disenchanted with a denominational church and didn't
really understand the meaning of salvation until
joining The Local Church in his city. Now he realizes that The Local Church has the real truth while
the denomination he left wallows in error and
corruption.

Members submit to a strong authority structure
of elders. A family may need approval for trading
a car, changing jobs, or moving to another locality.
Russell T. Hitt, consulting editor of *Eternity,* knows
of one Local Church member ordered by his spir-

itual authority to leave his wife and children in California and move to Chicago.

Partly because of the search for security and authority today, The Local Church is growing. Already there are congregations in 30 U.S. cities, with more being established as groups of 50-100 members move to new locations under direction of their spiritual authorities.

Three recent converts are former Southern Baptist ministers. One is longtime Southern Baptist evangelist and pastor Jerry Reimer, a graduate of Oklahoma Baptist University and Southwestern Baptist Theological Seminary. "I have terminated my Southern Baptist life and returned my ordination certificate," he says, "and am now brand new in a brand new thing."

The Body A nomadic gaggle of robed youth hikes from one college campus to another, existing on handouts and stale food discarded by stores. "New souls" stumble along with bowed heads so they will not be tempted by enticing billboard pictures and window displays. Singles are segregated by sex and dare not look at any part of the opposite sex's body except the feet. Married women always plod several paces behind their husbands.

Members of this ascetic band of perhaps less than a hundred are told it is sinful to lay up any treasures on earth. They are forbidden to contact parents and former friends. They may read only the Bible, hymnals, and a few approved recipe books.

The Church Another group of hitchhiking, train-hopping nomads, is led by an ex-Marine named Jim Roberts, who calls himself "Brother Evangelist." One youth reportedly walked 12,000 miles, carrying a Bible, wearing only a robe and sandals, sleeping under bridges and in parks, and eating out of garbage cans, "in search of the Lord," and gave "Brother Evangelist" $2,200.

Thirty-two members of Roberts' flock were riding in a flatbed truck that turned over near Fayetteville, Arkansas injuring several and killing a five-month-old girl. One member who has since left the group recalls that the "brothers" set his broken arm because they did not believe in doctors.

Brother Julius' Followers The leader is said to call himself the "Second Coming of Christ" and his devoted followers "Angels in the Flesh." He appears to hold a spellbinding grip on them. A sorrowing Connecticut mother says her 18-year-old daughter fainted on first meeting him, and at his request immediately gave up all her belongings in exchange for a Bible. She then dropped out of high school six weeks before graduation and left home. A few months later the mother heard that Julius had "married" his followers by lining the boys up on one side and girls on the other and having them choose partners.

One of his most devoted worshipers is a New York City school teacher. Charged with luring students into the cult, she steadfastly refuses to quit her job.

Bishop Devernon LeGrand's Church The "Bishop" and one of his sons were imprisoned for the 1975 rape of a young woman they reportedly held prisoner in their church building. More recently, the "Reverend Doctor," as the leader is also called, was charged with the beating deaths of two sisters whose bodies were recovered from a lake near the church's camp in the Catskills. The sisters,

16 and 18, and other female members had been posing as nuns to solicit money for the church.

And there are still more. The Christian Freedom Foundation lists over 60 cultic groups to which parents have lost children. Their beliefs vary. Their methods of recruiting and holding members are often tragically similar: enticement by a mesmerizing leader who claims divinity or discovery of exclusive religious truth, submission and surrender of money and property to him, indoctrination that appears to border on brainwashing, and absorption into a tightly knit group who cling to one another and the leader in fear and insecurity.

Some are more weird and bizarre than others. All deviate from traditional Christian doctrine and practice.

11

Why All the Fuss?

From his 10-year-study of "fringe religious cults," University of Chicago anthropologist Irving Zaretsky concludes that up to 20 million Americans may be involved. *U.S. News and World Report* puts the number at three million, mostly in their teens or early 20s. A recent Gallup poll indicates that about 12 percent of American young adults are presently "engaged in nontraditional religious movements."

Yet, according to a *Minneapolis Tribune* survey, most people think the new cults are no cause for alarm. As for their young followers, "When they get older, they will go back to established religion," commented a postal employee. One out of five persons thinks such groups as Moon's Unification Church offer youth "deep spiritual involvement."

Parents who have lost children to cults are more likely to side with the worried minority in the Minneapolis poll. They tend to agree with the

Minnesotan who said, "It [cultism] is a serious, dangerous conspiracy to corrupt the young."

Three arguments are generally given by those espousing a nonalarmist position over the new expressions of cultism. They generally express half-truths.

1. *All Christian denominations were considered radical in their beginnings.*

The Protestant Reformers initially saw themselves as housecleaners within the Roman Catholic Church. Luther, for example, never wanted to leave the fold, but was excommunicated as an heretical troublemaker.

Inevitably, major schismatic bodies developed— principally the Lutheran, Calvinist (Presbyterian), and Church of England denominations. Within states controlled by Protestant and Catholic hierarchies, Free Church forerunners of Baptists, Mennonites, and other congregational democracies arose.

For practicing believers' baptism, opposing religiopolitico laws, and refusing to pay tithes, nonconformist believers were severely persecuted in Europe and later in colonial America. The Baptist "radicals" were primarily responsible for the formulation and ratification of the First Amendment, which guarantees Americans constitutional rights to the freedom of religion, speech, the press, and the right of petition.

However, the radical nature of Christian denominations related primarily to new structure and the need for reforms, not to basic doctrine. The Protestant and Free Church movements continued in the stream of historic Christianity in accepting the inspiration of the Bible, the sinfulness of man, the

Trinitarian Godhead, and Jesus' atonement on the cross for sin.

The modern cults are radical both in origin and in departure from traditional Christian beliefs. The Hinduistic and consciousness-raising cults accept none of the basic tenets of Christianity as unique. And the Christian heresies diverge from historical Christianity at major points.

2. *During the past two milleniums cults have come and gone. Those that have survived became domesticated within society. The modern cults will follow this pattern.*

This argument contains just enough truth to mislead most Westerners.

Cults, like shooting stars, do keep appearing and disappearing. Some have moved into the mainstream of society. Some have remained outside.

The Mormons belong in the first category. Once regarded as radical and subversive, mainly because of their practice of polygamy (dropped in 1890), Mormons are today extolled for industry, thrift, wholesome family life, and educational and artistic excellence. Mormons serve in the U.S. Senate and the cabinet; a Mormon could probably now be elected president as easily as a Catholic.

Jehovah's Witnesses are less accepted. This is not because they deny the Trinity and say Jesus is only an angel who became a man. (Certain Mormon beliefs are also considered heretical by the Catholic Church and Protestant denominations.) Jehovah's Witnesses remain suspect because they have declared themselves a theocratic nation, subject only to God's laws as they interpret them, above society. They disdain blood transfusions, decline to salute the flag, and refuse to serve in a national army. A Witness is not likely ever to be elected president.

Under new leadership, modern cults such as the Children of God might conceivably melt into the mainstream of society as the Mormons have. However it is difficult to believe that groups such as the Church of Armageddon will ever conform. And it is more incredible to assume that the occultic and Hinduistic groups will ever move into the spectrum of historic Christianity.

3. *All religious groups recruit, indoctrinate, and train their members. The new cults are only more aggressive, intense, and thorough. In time they will become less so as older religions have.*

Religious groups do grow and become vital by evangelizing, discipling, and training members to reproduce themselves. Christian scholars who believe that the real Church can never be destroyed recognize that forms and structures function by sociological laws. The Church is eternal while "churches" are temporal.

So Presbyterian churches ask joiners to "submit" to the spiritual authority of elected elders. The Catholic hierarchy expects its constituency to obey laws proclaimed by official church councils and the papal "vicar of Christ" when he speaks of faith and morals. And congregationally governed bodies such as Baptists have church covenants to which members subscribe.

However, thoughtful Christians devoted to the biblical concept of soul liberty will not use questionable methods of persuasion and conversion. Nor will they misuse spiritual authority and group pressure to keep persons within the fold.

There is no doubt that in many respects the cults

are different in origin, belief, and practice from mainline church bodies. When their inner workings are carefully studied, there does appear to be cause for alarm.

Let us now consider the major "offenses" which parent groups and others attribute to cults in varying degrees.

Violation of tax-exempt status Angry parents speaking at the Washington Day of Affirmation and Protest called on government officials to investigate the tax exemptions of cults, and in particular the status of the Unification Church.

Rep. Peter A. Peyser, whose home adjoins UC property in Tarrytown, New York, responded that high-level Internal Revenue Service officials were already probing Moon's operations. Several "obvious questions" were involved, he said, particularly those focusing on the church's political activities, fund-raising, and property acquisition.

Questionable exemptions granted cults is part of the muddled tax situation relating to religious groups. The IRS has stirred up a tempest by asking religious organizations to file financial information on their "integrated auxiliaries." These the IRS defines as church-related schools, hospitals, orphanages, and such. It is not only the fear of losing tax exemption that has upset church leaders, but the attempt by government to define the nature and mission of a church.

But can the churches opposed to cults have their tax-exempt "cake" while asking the IRS to deny any frosting to the objectionable cults? If so, the government would have to divide religions into approved and disapproved categories. This would obviously violate the First Amendment's guarantee of freedom of religion.

Fraudulent fund raising   The Unification Church, Hare Krishna, and the Children of God are charged with soliciting under false pretenses and violation of local ordinances requiring the filing of accurate financial statements for permits.

The use of front names and purposes—"Give to our drug prevention program," etc.—appears to be widely practiced. Says Dr. Samuel A. Jeanes, an alarmed Baptist pastor in New Jersey: "People must be protected against solicitation of funds in the name of religion or in the name of good causes such as campaigns against drugs and pornography that may or may not ever be launched. America has 'truth in advertising' laws as well as laws which deal with fraud which might be perpetrated on the public in the name of religion."

Ex-Moonie Cynthia Slaughter explained the rationalization she followed in deceptive fund raising:

In the Unification cult, two wrongs make a right. Because in the Garden of Eden, Satan deceived God's children. Now God's children—that is, the Unification Church members—are justified to deceive Satan, that is the Satan-controlled world.

This is called "heavenly deception." And I practiced this personally in my daily fund raising. I averaged $150 to $200 per day for a year and a half.

Money is also obtained from parents by dubious means.

A mother received a "frantic" phone call from her daughter, saying she desperately needed $3,000 in cash for some courses to help "overcome some problems." The mother sent $1,000 that night, indicating that the remainder would be sent later.

A few days later she learned that the money was for Scientology courses.

The N.Y. Attorney General's report on the Children of God described how "members, especially 'babes' are instructed . . . to write their parents for monies and supplies needed to run the commune." The father of one COG "babe" sent between $2,500 and $3,000. The checks were endorsed in her name and deposited to the commune's account. When she was sent away for refusing to ask her parents for more money, she reported never having seen any of the checks sent.

A third question relating to finances concerns profiteering by cult leaders. Moon lives in a mansion and sails on luxury yachts. Moses Berg is presumed to receive thousands of dollars from sales of literature on the streets. L. Ron Hubbard is said to get a substantial rake-off from Scientology fees. Large sums flow into the headquarters of Hare Krishna, the Divine Light Mission, and Transcendental Meditation enterprises. Most of the money is collected by ordinary members who may receive only a subsistence allowance for working from 12 to 18 hours a day.

As already mentioned, the IRS wants financial statements from "integrated auxiliaries" of churches. Other federal agencies are probing possible violation of the Fair Labor Standards Act of 1938. Says Ronald J. James, Administrator of the Wage and Hour Division of the Department of Labor, "I look with suspicion on those 'volunteers' who spend substantial—or all—of their time in 'voluntary' activities." Just how far such an investigation can be pressed remains to be seen. Again, the delicate matter of religious liberty is involved.

Blackmail of former members Cult opponents note that the Unification Church, COG, and Scientology ask new members to give confessional biographies of their past. Presumably these are kept on file, opening possibilities of use against defectors who are inclined to spill organizational secrets.

According to *Time*, this has made Scientology members susceptible to blackmail. *Time* cited a past Scientology policy of "'fair game,'" under which a defector could be "'deprived of property or injured by any means . . . sued, lied to, or destroyed.'" But the magazine also noted that Scientology's "worst practices" had been dropped (April 5, 1976).

Alienation of familial affections Like a broken record the story keeps repeating. A son or daughter joins a cult. Telephone calls home (always collect) are awkward and stiff. Pleas to come home are disregarded, even when a close relative becomes ill or dies. Heartbreak turns to anger, with parents often taking drastic steps to "recapture" their child. If the parents fail, as most do, communication is cut off and they can only seethe in frustration and lament the loss of their flesh and blood.

Probably tens of thousands of parents have had such an experience. Rabbi Maurice Davis of White Plains, New York, a leader of a parent group, says his organization alone has received over a thousand letters from parents heartbroken "in the deepest degree" over losing their kids to the Unification Church.

The UC and COG are known to twist Bible passages to turn youths against their parents. A member wanting to go home to a family funeral may be shown Matthew 8:22—Jesus said to a disciple, "Follow Me; and let the dead bury their dead."

How do the "Christian" cults get around biblical commands for children to honor and obey their parents? Moses Berg explains: "The Bible talks about obeying your parents in the Lord (which is your leadership, not your ungodly fleshly parents). It says obey them in all things, even if they are wrong! If a leader tells you to do something wrong you are justified before God for obeying leadership. . . ."

Cults of Eastern origin use other ploys for driving a wedge between members and disapproving parents.

"They (Krishna devotees) convinced me that my parents were a bad influence," recalls Robin George of Cypress, California, who was drawn into Krishna at 15 and shunted from city to city while her parents searched frantically for her.

The cults, of course, deny alienating members from their parents. "The Moonies will try to help you patch up family relations, although their intentions may be only to get your parents into the church," says pianist John Spradling. His parents didn't contest his involvement in the Unification Church. If they had, would his superiors have said they were of Satan? "Yes, definitely," he concedes.

The reaction of the cults appears to hinge on parental attitudes. If parents hold a positive or even a neutral stance, they may be able to maintain some communication with children. If they become negative, their children are likely to be told they are of Satan or of *maya*.

Brainwashing (also called "menticide," mind manipulation and mind alteration) This is the "red flag" charge which has aroused the deepest and most intense concern about the new cults.

Brainwashing as a method of control has undoubtedly been used by tyrants and zealots of all ages. As a science it is a modern phenomenon, dating from experiments performed on dogs by Ivan Pavlov (1849-1936), a Russian surgeon, physiologist, and experimental psychologist.

Pavlov, who won a Nobel Prize in 1904 for his work on the physiology of the digestive glands, proved in other experiments that behavior patterns could be altered in dogs by electric shock treatments and environmental changes. He showed that a dog could be conditioned to hate what it previously loved and vice versa.

After Pavlov's death, Communist psychologists built on his research to develop a system for the "reeducation of human masses." Communist brainwashing techniques have since been used most successfully on a mass scale in China.

The new Chinese revolutionary government first aroused guilt and anxiety over past behavior by propaganda campaigns and personal accusations, including denunciations of parents by children. Millions joined in orgies of group repentance until they were conditioned for "knee-jerk" response to commands of the Party.

The dynamic in brainwashing did not hit home to Americans until the prisoner exchange in Korea that marked the end of hostilities there in 1953. Some American POWs refused repatriation saying they wished to live under Communism. When others arrived home, families noticed marked changes in attitudes and personal behavior reflecting Communist ideology. Interviews revealed that many of the POWs had been starved, frozen, removed from associations with companions, constantly questioned and badgered, then offered peace and comfort if they would write confessions and surrender to Communist thought patterns.

The reports raised such a hubbub that the UN General Assembly adopted a general resolution condemning brainwashing as it had been practiced by the Communists.

Four years later British psychiatrist William Sargent published his epochal book on brainwashing, *Battle for the Mind.* Basing his research principally on records from the 18th century Wesleyan revivals and on Communist techniques, Sargent concluded that the possibilities of brainwashing were so far reaching that, "the politico-religious struggle for the mind of man may well be won by whoever becomes most conversant with the normal and abnormal functions of the brain, and is readiest to make use of the knowledge gained." (Harper and Row Publications, Inc., 1971.)

Sargent was attacked by some religious leaders for presuming that conversion could be explained psychologically, though he stated that he was "not concerned with the truth or falsity of . . . (Christian) beliefs," but "only with the physiology of conversion and thought control." He felt that "a better understanding of the means of creating and consolidating faith will enable religious bodies to expand much more rapidly."

Sargent noted that the British author of a book on Chinese Communism had described six factors present in Communist training methods: isolation from family and former friends, fatigue, memorizing "great amounts of theoretical material" and use of new terminology, tension with uncertainty of success, use of vicious language, and the forbidding of humor.

This, Sargent noted, led to "acute crisis and breakdown" during which the process called "tail-cutting"—severing of ties with old values, family and friends—takes place. The convert is "now fired with the conviction that he must publicize his newly found security and help others find peace of mind through service to the Organization." After "another four months of intense work to consolidate the hold on the now willing mind," the new Communist man goes forth with other dedicated missionaries to organize discussion and confession groups all over China.*

Cult opponents contend that the Unification Church, Hare Krishna, the Children of God, Scientology, and other alleged control groups use basically many of the same techniques employed by the Communists—in vying for different ideological ends, of course. In support, they cite opinions of various experts in the mental health field who have interviewed and examined former cult members.

Dr. Marvin F. Galper, a practicing clinical psychologist in San Diego, described the cultic "brainwashing process" in a paper presented at the 1976 meeting of the Tampa-St. Petersburg-Clearwater Psychiatric Society:

The cult seeks to surround the potential recruit with its own socially isolated subculture in which external reality feedback from the outside envi-

---

*pp. 71-72 cited by Sargent from *China Under Communism* by R. L. Walker (London: Allen & Unwin, 1956).

ronment is inaccessible to the indoctrinee. Suppression of the individual's rational judgment processes is fostered by sleep deprivation and sensory bombardment. Mobilization of guilt and anxiety in the indoctrinee intensifies this inhibition of judgmental processes and at the same time leads to heightened suggestibility. The cult environment has a basically regressive thrust. A childlike ego state is fostered in the individual. He is constantly manipulated and molded by skillfully applied methods of indirect suggestion.

Dr. Galper then explained the results in terms of psychic functioning.

The value hierarchy of the cult member undergoes marked alteration. The frequently seen abandonment of previously held academic and career goals by brainwashed college students provides dramatic evidence in this regard. Cognitive flexibility and adaptability are reduced. One also sees narrowing and blunting in the range of consciously experienced effect. The conscious experience of the mind-control victim is laden with shallow "programmed-in" cult effects. He is preoccupied with "programmed-in" cult ideologies and cult fantasies. Deep and genuine love feelings undergo repression to varying degrees. Frequent severence of established lifelong ties with parents and family or origin is indicative of the overall dehumanizing impact of the cult environment.

Mrs. Jean Merrit, testifying for a group of mental health professionals at the Day of Affirmation and Protest, declared:

We definitely believe that brainwashing, mind control, persuasive coercion is occurring. We see very obvious common denominators where you can have five people from five different parts of this country coming out and saying the exact same thing, word for word. The technique used in brainwashing is exactly the same, whether it be Reverend Moon's Unification movement . . . the Hare Krishna movement . . . [or] anything else.

The techniques. The words. "Love." We associate "love" as being warm fuzzies. What they are told "love" means is when you are out fund-raising, you "Love someone up." What that means is that you go up to them and act in satanical ways, if necessary . . . But you "love" them to get that dollar; you get that donation for the candy . . . We would call it "conning" the public. You'd "love them up" by telling them you were raising money for a drug rehab center. We would interpret that in our terminology as, "you are conning the people; you are lying."

Support for the charge that psychic damage is inflicted comes from the high number of cult-member trauma cases, including a number of questionable deaths. Harvard psychiatrist John Clark, Jr. testified in District of Columbia Superior Court that the ex-Moonies he had examined appeared physically and emotionally exhausted. "A few were psychotic," he said.

District Attorney Albert Rosenblatt of Duchess County, New York, in which the UC training center is located, wonders why so many Moonies come to a local hospital for emergency-room treatment.

Perhaps the most telling testimonies come from ex-cultists about their experiences. The following statements are typical of hundreds which the parents' groups have on file:

Julie Kimes of Allison Park, Pa. claims she was "psychologically kidnapped" out of college by the Children of God. "Cult members," she says, "become convinced they are living the life God has chosen for them, that any other life is wrong, and God will retaliate against anyone who leaves."

Chuck Pinson of Atlanta, a former elder in COG for four and one-half years, declares, "It's the same technique as Korean brainwashing. . . . The cult groups use a combination of mental pressure and exhaustion to wear down their young converts."

Janis Feiden of San Antonio, a former "trusted sister" in the UC, believes she was "a programmed robot. By the time I had completed my training, the lecturers had indoctrinated me to the point where I believed that Moon was God and that he would produce a Master Race and save the world."

Still, responsible persons can be found who disagree. One who thinks that brainwashing by the cults "is implying too much" is Berkeley Rice, a senior editor of *Psychology Today*. However, Rice concedes that much of the procedure follows the "classic steps of brainwashing": isolating people from outside influences, surrounding them with new supporting comrades and a new authority figure; wearing them down physically, mentally, and emotionally; then programming them with a new belief system and pressuring them into total commitment. But Moon's people do not "force anyone to join or believe," he adds, and "no one has proved" members are held against their will. Many parents and ex-Moonies would argue this last assertion.

Naturally, leaders of cults deny that brainwashing takes place. Neil Salonen, president of the U.S. branch of Moonism, claims "parents are being duped by an organized propaganda effort on the brainwashing issue. . . . Experiences in the (UC) church have been distorted."

More and more brainwashing-related cases against cults are coming to court. One action pending in Minnesota involves a parental suit against The Way International for alienation of a daughter's affection. Another against the UC in the superior Court of the District of Columbia has already been decided in favor of the defendant. The judge ruled that UC uses no method of teaching not used by other churches.

Because the court route is so slow and stands a good chance of being self-defeating, many parents have resorted to luring away or forcibly removing children for deprogramming from the physical premises of religious organizations.

What are the ethics of such actions? What are other responses to cults? We will examine these questions in the next chapter.

12

What Can Be Done?

The agony of parents who have "lost" children to cults cannot be adequately described.

Some have died in heartbreak. Others have had nervous breakdowns or heart attacks from worrying about their children. Many have spent their life savings for trips across the country and other expenses in desperate efforts to recover their children.

Some have made futile trips to court. These parents are thinking not just of their own emptiness or guilt over how they might have failed their children, but also of the years they believe their children are wasting and the damages being inflicted on youthful bodies and psyches.

One couple, for example, found their honor society son in a Hare Krishna dorm, ill from the flu, "lying on the floor of a cold and drafty room. . . . A bucket of juice with a common dipper was at the door for him and four others, also lying on the floor. The bathroom across from the 'sick room' had only a urinal and the floor was wet with urine. . . ."

After failing to recover their son, these parents saw him later on a Hollywood street passing out Krishna tracts. "Upon seeing us he started trembling, backed away, and shouted at us in anger, 'Stay away from me! Stay away from me!' . . . He acted like a frightened animal, cornered and growling a warning that he would or could fight to protect himself if necessary."

One difficulty is that parents have been slow to realize initially what their children are getting into. Ex-cultists say that the first few days are critical, that they might then have been dissuaded from further involvement with little difficulty. By the time the parents realize that the "educational foundation" or "Bible study group" is a cult, the youth is hooked.

Parents who are unaware of the differences between cults and conventional churches may feel that the cult is only a passing interest. After a time they realize their son or daughter is not coming home or going back to college soon, and they begin charting a course of action.

During the early '70s when the cults were little-known, parents hesitated to go public. They felt a sense of personal failure and were too embarrassed to let acquaintances know. Perhaps they talked to their pastor, if they had one, or a lawyer, and were told to wait or that nothing could be done. After waiting a few weeks, they began trying to track down their son or daughter. Many traveled across the country to be told their child was in another city or had left the country. And if their child was there they were allowed to see him only a short time and this in the presence of an older cult member.

FREECOG, the first "parent" organization, was seen as heaven-sent. Those who had youth in the Children of God were quickly reinforced by parents with children in Hare Krishna, the Unification Church, and other cults.

FREECOG's strongest ally was Ted Patrick, who had almost lost a nephew to COG. Still on the California governor's staff, Patrick had been begging state officials to heed parental complaints. Getting nowhere, he resigned to devote full time to "deprogramming" young cult members.

Deprogramming, as Patrick developed it, was essentially a two-step process. First, the cult member was removed from the cult on some pretense and transported to a house or motel room where other cultists could not get at him. He might be told a parent was sick or he might be invited to dinner. Once away from the environment of the cult, he would be taken by his parents and others —forcibly if necessary—to the deprogramming place.

There Patrick would conduct a marathon "counter-brainwashing" session lasting until the subject "broke." This might take one day, two, even a week or more.

A few subjects escaped, but most were persuaded to recant and to leave the cult. Some of those deprogrammed became Patrick's assistants and went on to become successful deprogrammers themselves.

Patrick was a lone wolf, but FREECOG promoted him in their newsletter and some parents gave him financial support. His fees ran up to $1,500 per case, not exorbitant because it included travel and motel expenses and sometimes a week or more of his time.

FREECOG evolved into the broader based Citizen's Freedom Foundation (CFF) with the avowed purpose "to alert the public and individuals to the problem of the misuse of mind-control techniques practiced by perverted and malevolent individuals who exploit others for personal satisfaction and financial gain."

CFF provided a list of helpful *Do's and Don'ts* for parents with children in cults.

Do record all names, addresses, phone numbers of persons known to be associated in any way with your child's activities.

Do establish and continue an association with an organized group of parents with similar problems.

Do maintain a written chronolog of events associated with your child's activities relating to the group.

Do answer all communications from your child in sincere, firm, but unrecriminating language.

Do collect related items from newspapers, magazines and other sources.

Do keep your "cool," avoid threats, be firm but open for communication at all times.

Do file a written complaint with your county supervisor and other public officials.

Do not feel guilty or alone. This is a common problem faced by thousands of parents all over this nation. It affects families of all religious, economic, and family backgrounds.

Do not send money to your child or to the group; without economic support the group cannot survive.

Do not give original documents to ANY party (unless required by law); provide copies ONLY.

Do not be persuaded by "professionals" to spend large amounts of money for "treatments" or legal action, until you have verified their credentials and qualifications for handling YOUR problem.

Do not give up; remember your child is a product of your love, training, heredity, and home environment. These influences can never be permanently eliminated by any techniques.

As the cults grew, other parents' organizations arose across the country.

In the Dallas-Fort Worth area, Cynthia Slaughter, the ex-debutante who had been deprogrammed out of the Unification Church, helped start the International Foundation for Individual Freedom (IFIF). Miss Slaughter was elected chairperson.

In Greensboro, North Carolina friends helped Mr. and Mrs. Aiden French, who had two daughters in Moonism, set up Citizens Organized for Public Awareness of Cults (COPAC). At COPAC's first public meeting over 300 persons filled St. Paul Presbyterian Church to hear ex-cult members describe how they had been "brainwashed."

In White Plains, New York Rabbi Maurice Davis and Dr. George W. Swope, an American Baptist minister and college guidance counselor, spearheaded the formation of Citizens Engaged in Reuniting Families (CERF).

These and other parent groups shared FREE-COG's purpose of alerting the public to what the cults were doing. As Anna Pace, the president of COPAC, put it, "Society has been lulled into believing the cults are harmless. They are not interested in saving souls. They're enslaving souls."

CERF formed the ad hoc committee which promoted the 1976 Day of Affirmation and Protest in Washington, D.C. They were supported by 14,000 Kansans petitioning Senator Robert Dole to investigate the web of elusive Moon fronts. Dole reserved a Senate hearing room and presided.

The unofficial hearing focused national attention on the methods of cultism for the first time. It also led to the forming of a second ad hoc committee, Committee Engaged in Freeing Minds (CEFM) to coordinate the work of CEF, IFIF, COPAC, and three other regional groups, Volunteer Parents of America of Torrence, California; Free Minds of Minneapolis; and Return to Personal Choice of Lincoln, Mass.

Besides providing public information and helping families, the umbrella committee intended to:

—Initiate investigations by government bodies of fraudulent and illegal activities of cults.

—Obtain court decisions recognizing the right of the individual to be free of mental coercion and hypnosis and making it illegal (a criminal offense) to control another's mind.

—Establish and maintain rehabilitation centers, professionally staffed, to reorient ex-cultists and return them to a normal life.

The term *deprogramming* is now avoided because of adverse publicity. The activity continues, however, and Patrick, though now in jail, is still seen as the savior of cult victims. "Black Lightning," as cult leaders call him, claims to have deprogrammed more than 1,000 young cultists in the past five years.

The legal battles over deprogramming center around alleged abductions of young people from cults and holding them against their will while the deprogrammer gives them a mental battering. Patrick's defense was presented by his attorney in a U.S. District Court where he was charged with aiding in the abduction of Kathy Crampton from the Church of Armageddon. The defense is based on Blackstone's "choice of evils" doctrine, a legal argument which John Ehrlichman cited in defending Richard Nixon.

Patrick's attorney contended that "the parents of Kathy Crampton, for whom and with whom Patrick acted, reasonably believed that the physical seizure and subsequent transportation of their daughter was necessary in order to avoid a harm greater than that sought to be avoided, in this case, by the kidnap statute."

He cited Section 3:02 in the U.S. Model Penal Code to this effect and an accompanying comment:

Property may be destroyed to prevent the spread of a fire. A speed limit may be violated in pursuing a suspected criminal. An ambulance may pass a traffic light. Mountain climbers lost in a storm may take refuge in a house or may appropriate provisions. . . .

Then he described the living conditions in the Armageddon commune, the drug use, and how Kathy had allegedly been changed into a "zombie."

He won an acquittal.

The same defense was successfully presented in a New York case of a different nature. There Patrick was charged with both assault and kidnapping. The incident involved the abduction of Dan Voll, a former Yale undergraduate who belonged to the small, tightly knit New Testament Missionary Fellowship (NTMF). Unlike Patrick's usual cultic targets, the NTMF held to evangelical doctrine and the members lived apart and worked at regular jobs. Their main deviation from traditional worship appeared to be a ritual called "dancing in the Spirit," a lively, solo two-step expressing spiritual joy. But their critics claimed they were elitist and put the Fellowship ahead of family ties.

Voll's parents had disapproved of his decision not to study for the Lutheran ministry as previously planned, and his failure to come home the previous Christmas. They were also disappointed that he had taken a leave of absence from Yale to help in the NTMF's minuscule publishing enterprise.

Just 13 days before young Voll's 21st birthday, his parents and Patrick grabbed him on a New York street and hustled him into a waiting car. The youth called for help, and police stopped the car before they had gone two blocks. The abductors were arrested.

Voll's former college roommate, Wes Lockwood, who had been earlier deprogrammed out of the NTMF, testified for the defense. He said he had not thought independently during his two and one-half years in the group and that he now favored Patrick's rescue technique.

President William McGill of Columbia University, which employed several Fellowship members, called them "perfectly fine young people." Even if they were "repellent," he "would not tolerate any acts restricting young people."

Dean Kelley, staff associate for religious and civil

liberties of the National Council of Churches, also praised the Fellowship, saying that without such "high demand" religious groups some youths might turn to drugs, crime, even commit suicide.

First the judge dismissed the assault charge against Patrick. Then he instructed the jury on the "choice of evils" provision in the penal code. Again, Patrick was pronounced not guilty.

Patrick's luck ran out in Colorado where he was accused of abducting a Hare Krishna devotee. A Denver judge placed him on probation on condition that he not become involved in any more kidnappings. Later he was arrested in Orange County, California on a similar charge involving a Krishna member. The California judge ordered that he begin serving a one-year term, including a 60-day probation violation sentence stemming from the Denver conviction. Patrick claimed afterward that he had not been allowed to explain at the trial that the Krishna girl was already at her parents' home when he was asked to talk with her.

After Patrick went to prison, a Superior Court Judge in Los Angeles ruled that the parents of the Krishna girl had committed an "illegal act" in seizing and holding their daughter for deprogramming. The judge said the girl, who had escaped into police custody, could rejoin her temple pending possible criminal action against her family. Her mother sobbed, "I just want my daughter, I love my daughter."

The legal risks entailed in kidnapping children have spurred a search for other means of getting them away from the influence of their cultic persuaders. Some parents have been successful in obtaining court orders remanding an adult child into their custody for a specified time to get professonal help.

Edwin Taylor, of North Carolina got such a warrant to remove his son from a group called "The Way, The Truth, The Life" for confinement to a hospital. The boy had been in the group for only three days and he didn't recognize his father when he came out. The boy's "rehabilitation" took five days.

In Washington, D.C. a couple obtained a warrant from Superior Court Judge Nicholas Nunzio for the removal of their 22-year-old son from the Unification Church. The parents, accompanied by a U.S. park policeman, found the youth at Moon's Bicentennial Washington Monument rally and took him away for deprogramming.

But such court orders are given at a judge's discretion, and there have been conflicting court decisions. Some parents have been simply instructed that the First Amendment blocks any such recourse. Likely the controversy will go all the way to the U.S. Supreme Court.

Even when parents are successful in removing their child from a cult, deprogramming may not succeed. The youth may escape during the process or later be overcome by guilt feelings and return to the cult. Communication then becomes practically impossible.

One of the saddest such incidents involved the Aiden French family—Mr. and Mrs. French helped found COPAC.

The tragedy began when their oldest daughter, Rhonda, an airline stewardess and former Sunday School teacher, joined the Unification Church in San Francisco. After many exasperating phone calls and her failure to come home for her grandmother's funeral, they sought Ted Patrick's help.

They got her out to go "sightseeing," then forcibly transported her south to Long Beach for deprogramming by Patrick. The next morning they let her out of sight just once. She quickly climbed through a small bathroom window and ran to a nearby highway. There she hitchhiked a ride before her father could catch her.

A second attempt made by Mrs. French failed when she could not locate Rhonda. The third time two young men helped Mrs. French find her and get her into a car. But before they could drive away, several Moonies jerked open the doors and took her back.

Rhonda's younger sister, Nelda, who had often spoken strongly against Moonism, offered to help. With much misgiving, Mrs. French permitted Nelda to visit Rhonda at the UC's "New Ideal Ranch" about 70 miles from San Francisco. When Nelda failed to return to the city as agreed, Mrs. French got a police escort and went to the farm. A glassy-eyed Nelda met her, saying "Moon is our teacher now," and refused to leave. The policeman told Mrs. French, "She's of age. You can't make her go."

Such sorrow is felt by many other parents whose children will not see them alone because they fear kidnapping. On the other hand, parents object to seeing their children in front of other cult members who they say are intimidating.

To alleviate anxiety on both sides, New York City police have designated a special meeting place for Moon youth and their parents at the Midtown South Precinct, a block from the Moonies' Hotel

New Yorker. The police guarantee the Moonies they will not be kidnapped. And if one decides to return home, the police will not permit interference from other Moonies.

Apart from the difficulties involved in getting a child away from a cultic commune, some deep ethical objections are raised against the deprogramming process. Opponents say that deprogrammers:

—Decide for themselves what is or is not a valid religious group.

—Assume that the parents' religious or non-religious faith deserves more state protection than that of their adult child.

—Pose as experts when they have little, if any, training in psychology.

—Conduct an inquisition.

—Deprive youth of religious liberty.

—Practice one evil to counteract another evil.

—Leave the deprogrammed youth burned out and cynical of all belief systems.

Defenders of deprogramming say those objecting don't understand how far the cults go in short-circuiting reason and annihilating both thought and consequent emotion. William O. West, a representative of the IFIF parents' group, wrote in *Eternity* (September, 1976):

Deprogramming aims at breaking the chains of fear, guilt, and repetitive thought, and at forcing objective evaluation of the unexamined beliefs that were injected into the victim's unresisting mind by the cult leaders after the behavioral chains were originally established. The examination of what the person already believes is the deprogrammer's goal, rather than trying to force him to adopt a new belief. Deprogramming neutralizes the mind. . . . The process does not involve any alternative behavioral programming. . . . West concedes that deprogramming must of necessity include a dramatic, and hopefully shocking, presentation of alternative interpretations of specific phenomena. If a deprogrammer can induce his subject to attempt to defend his cult against charges for which he does not have previously memorized answers, the subject will be forced to think and, eventually, to recognize that he has accepted, on blind faith, certain ideas which are contrary to biblical teachings, and certainly open to question. At this point it is customary to read aloud Matthew 24 and to consider the possibility that the leader of his particular cult is not the Messiah, a reincarnated prophet, or the "handmaiden of the Lord," as these self-appointed demagogues invariably claim.

Before his own deprogramming, West was a member of the Divine Light Mission. Members of the evangelical Berkeley Christian Coalition tried to convert him to Christ and failed. "My mind was completely closed to such." After being deprogrammed, his mind became "free to explore other objections," he says, although "my deprogrammer was not interested in converting me to orthodox Christianity (or to anything else)." When Coalition members talked to him again he was able to "gratefully accept Jesus Christ as my personal Saviour."

Understandably, deprogramming is viewed with alarm by small high-demand evangelical groups. Moishe Rosen, leader of Jews for Jesus, has prepared for his group written instructions on dealing with deprogrammers. "It is not hard," Rosen says, "for Jewish parents to believe that their children were 'brainwashed' into accepting Christ."

The few conservative evangelical leaders who have spoken out tend to be against deprogramming. Dr. J. C. Macaulay, for example, president of the New York School of the Bible, thinks the parents' groups "mean well. But the end doesn't justify the means. I wouldn't want anyone trying to take away my faith, so I shouldn't be trying to take away another's faith. These new cults have the wrong answers, but I still would respect the decision of young people to follow Moon, even if they believe he is the Messiah. They are of age."

On the West coast, the head of the Berkeley Christian Coalition, Bill Squires, argues that deprogramming is, in effect, throwing out the baby with the bathwater. "It seems to dismantle a person's whole ideological structure, which can be seriously damaging to the personality. I know personally some deprogrammed people who, when approached with the Gospel, respond, 'Well, it sounds very good, but how do I know you are not just trying to program me again?' . . . So they are extremely cynical and very, very cautious. They feel that they have been ripped off once by something they considered to be an ultimate spiritual reality and they are not going to be taken again. So it kind of cripples them in response to a real redemption."

What if Squires had a son or daughter in the Unification Church or any other cult? "Well, I guess I'd pray a lot, and keep communications open from my end."

So the controversy rages over the drastic steps which thousands of desperate parents have taken to try to get their children out. But is any other help available?

Professional rehabilitative services are opening to parents and ex-cult members. The pioneer in the field is Return to Personal Choice of Newton, Massachusetts. Membership is restricted to mental health professionals, lawyers, and clergy who do not have close relatives involved with any cultish group. There are also affiliated groups of psychiatrists and psychologists in Texas, Minnesota, Pennsylvania, and New York.

Former cultists volunteer for treatment. Most have already been "deprogrammed" and need special therapy. "They've had to lie to their friends and family, and they have an awful lot of guilt," explains Jean Merritt, the psychiatric social worker who helped establish Return. "Or they were recruiters and when they see what they've done, they feel guilty."

Return also counsels parents who have children still in cults. "Parents wonder what they did wrong," says Mrs. Merritt. "We try to help them understand that, sure, sometimes parents make mistakes, but that often the kids don't know what they're joining. And we encourage the family to maintain a normal life to prevent them from being totally consumed by their involvement with a child."

Three evangelical groups are providing information and other assistance to persons who wish to compare cult doctrines with authentic biblical teaching.

Christians United for Jesus as Lord is a loose coalition of concerned Christians from 31 churches and affiliated organizations in New York City. Because Moonism is the most active cult in this area, they are concentrating on the Unification Church.

Members of Christians United have distributed literature outside Moon rallies in Manhattan and have spoken to churches and other groups. They also assist youth who wish to leave the UC.

The most active members of Christians United belong to Calvary Baptist Church. Because Christians United has no office, Calvary staff and members receive calls and mail out information.

Being near the local Moon headquarters and the New Yorker Hotel, Calvary Church is easily accessible to disenchanted Moonies seeking a Christian alternative.

Michael Scott was referred to Calvary Church by the local Crisis Center. An assistant team leader of a fund-raising team, he had become disillusioned with Moon after one of his friends committed suicide (the Moonie who lay down on a railroad track and was run over by a train).

> I had no money, no friends, no nothing, except for some clothes. I felt like a bird in a cage who couldn't get out. I could see and couldn't do anything. So I took a lethal overdose of sleeping pills and didn't even get a hangover. A couple of days later I called the help line. Because I was trusted my calls weren't monitored. The man who answered happened to be a Christian and referred me to Calvary Church, where I found God's love, forgiveness, and open arms. That very evening I left the Unification Church forever.

Another Moonie who found help at Calvary

Church is John Spradling, the talented young musician who had joined the Unification Church while studying piano in Austria. His superiors valued his talents and had allowed him to move near the Julliard School of Music, where he had enrolled. While reading the Bible alone he began to disbelieve much of what he had been taught in Moonism. "I decided I just had to go to a church and try to find salvation. I looked in the yellow pages and saw Calvary Church. I went and accepted Christ in the evening service."

Scott and Spradling have joined others in Christians United seeking to win Moonies to Christ. They do not favor deprogramming. "We simply show them love—that's how many got into the Unification Church in the first place—and then try to get them into the Bible."

On the West coast the Spiritual Counterfeits Project (SCP) and the Christian Research Institute (CRI) provide literature, cassette tapes, and speakers in their educational response to popular cults.

CRI, located in southern California, is headed by Dr. Walter R. Martin, long an authority on religious cults. The CRI has dealt mainly with Jehovah's Witnesses and other older cults, and is just beginning to investigate the newer aberrations. Says Robert L. Passantino, Research Associate, "It is certainly not our desire to personally condemn anyone. . . . It is our duty as Christians, however, to speak out against false doctrine."

SCP, a ministry of the Berkeley Christian Coalition, has developed the most wide-ranging repository of information on the newest occult, psychic, and mystical spiritual groups active in the U.S. today. The group publishes a newsletter for donors and other interested persons and offers their material, as does CRI, at nominal cost.

So some help is available for troubled cult members, parents, and others asking, "What can be done?"

13

Why Do the Cults Keep Growing?

If the Eastern swamis and gurus should all pack their bags and return to India; if Sun Myung Moon should go into permanent eclipse; if "Moses" Berg should drown in the Red Sea; if all the cults that plague Western society should suddenly fizzle— what then?

New groups would surely arise to fill the void and we would simply see a rerun of the same chaotic religious show.

It is not enough to expose the methods and doctrines of the cults, nor to prosecute those cult leaders who violate the law under the cloak of freedom of religion, nor to win present cult members back to ways more acceptable to their parents and society.

For the sake of future generations we must discover what makes our youth and others so vulnerable to the strange sirens of cultism.

This necessity is illustrated by an encounter between a mountaineer and a hiker from the city who was trying to get a drink of clear water from a muddy stream. "Stranger," the mountain man advised, "you'd do a heap better if you'd go up yonder and run the hogs out of the spring."

It is not hard to identify the "hogs" that are spoiling the stream of life for youth today.

1. *Family Problems.* "I've never seen one of these young people who didn't have some kind of serious failure in family life," says Dr. Herbert Hendin, a Columbia University psychoanalyst who studies youth movements for the Center for Policy Research. "They're turning desperately from the pain of the outside world to the childlike support and structures of a make-believe family" *(U. S. News and World Report,* June 14, 1976).

Testimonies of ex-cultists seem to bear this out.

"There was no meaningful communication at all within my family," recalls Des Carne, whose father holds a doctorate in etymology. Carne was involved in Krishna and other Eastern religions before becoming a Christian.

"We were never a close family," says Miriam McClendon, who returned to the Children of God after her divorced mother, a Texas college professor, had her committed to a hospital for treatment.

Arthur Robins, a talented artist, told his parents after he was deprogrammed that the Moonies got him to talk about childhood incidents, such as a time when he was two and one-half and his mother was too busy to hold him on her lap. "See, we're your family. We're the ones who love you," he says the Moonies told him.

Rabbi Maurice Davis has advised his congregation to face up to family needs which cults are exploiting.

We can [expose law violations of Moon] . . . and should. The question that keeps me awake at night, however, is why our kids—even a few of them—are so vulnerable. How is it possible that one weekend at Tarrytown can destroy a lifetime of family and values? For, believe me, it happens and who is there among us so secure that he would let his children go to Tarrytown, and be confident that nothing would happen?

What is the need that we do not fulfill? Our kids have all things material—and that simply is not enough. One boy said to me, "But now at least I believe in something. My parents believe in nothing."

Well, we are those parents, you and I. Most of us are fairly decent people. We work hard. We do the right thing. We have a set of values, and we try to live by them. What's missing? Is it that we do not speak enough about those values? Is it that we do not show enough of our love? Is it that we do not share with our children our deeper dreams, our deeper goals?

Our children want to believe in something. And if we do not help them, the Moon people will.

Then let us begin again . . . to listen with our ears and with our hearts. And let us bare our souls to our children, that they may know us for our dreams. Let us share our lives more openly without pretense, without defense, with a love that must not be denied.

I can give you a thousand reasons why we must do this and more. But who needs a thousand reasons? We are fighting for our children and their lives, and that—I suggest—is reason enough.

This is not to say that many families with children in cults failed to do the best they could. There are powerful forces in modern society which often counter the best intentions of parents, whose first reaction may be to blame themselves.

Job mobility and frequent transfers by companies have broken close ties with the extended family of grandparents, aunts, uncles, and cousins that was such a stabilizer for youth one-half century ago. Half of all U.S. family heads now live over 100 miles from where they were born. One in five resides more than a thousand miles from his birthplace.

Says Vance Packard in *A Nation of Strangers:* The people of America have no more urgent problem today than to combat the uprootedness and unconnectedness which is producing so much social fragmentation. Most can start in their own towns and urban neighborhoods. Technological progress is no bargain if we lose the natural human community in the process (New York: David McKay Company, Inc., 1972, p. 334).

Youth also face unrelenting peer pressure almost every waking hour of the day. With parents occupied by demands of jobs, commuting, and social pressures, children are left at the mercy of their peer groups in school, at play, on part-time jobs, and even in Sunday School, where they usually study away from parents. The few hours left for home communication are mostly taken by the telephone, television, and other distractions.

2. *Educational factors.* Public education is supposed to prepare young people for successful living. Instead it is having an undermining effect in some instances.

While youth once did adult work in their teens, today over half continue in school until 21 or 22 without meaningful involvement in a wage-earning occupation. And many pursue graduate studies into their late 20s. It is significant that the Moonies have been most successful in recruiting college students during this period of extended adolescence.

Also, the trend in education today is not to indoctrinate, as in the past, but to present options, arouse curiosity, and provoke questions. In the humanities nothing is considered absolute. Every moral choice is presented in a situational context with each individual left to determine what is best for him.

In this climate students still hunger for absolutes. As one told Billy Graham, "I feel like a ship at sea without a rudder."

Such students, thinks Catholic psychologist John Malecki, are wide open to the absolutist positions of cults like the Unification Church. "There is a whole generation of alienated youth that hungers for certain beliefs that are absolutes," he says. "Moon offers an anchor in a time of sociocultural revolution. Once you buy the idea that Moon is absolute, and it's a very powerful idea, you surrender your will to him. You become a puppet under the control of an absolutist."

A third factor in today's educational process is the sense of dehumanization and depersonalization

202 / The Youthnappers

which grips students on large campuses, where classes are often taught by teachers via closed-circuit television or by a graduate student assistant. Students are mere numbers. Many never build a personal relationship with even one of their professors.

The feeling of being a nonperson may persist into the vocational world. Cults have reached many young, idealistic workers who feel they are only cogs in a corporate or bureaucratic machine. "C'mon, you're spinning your wheels here," a Moon recruiter told a clerk in the U.S. Department of Agriculture. "Let me introduce you to people who know how to accomplish something in the world." The young bureaucrat instantly responded.

3. *Superficial romantic relationships.* Thousands of couples live together today with little more commitment than a pledge to share the apartment rent. Either one can get out whenever he or she wishes. Many other couples get married with the understanding that if it doesn't work out, they can opt for an amicable divorce.

What such young people don't realize is that breakups can leave one with deep emotional scars and a sense of worthlessness. As a young California divorcee put it, "I was bitter at people, lonely, and didn't know where I was going next. These [cult] people accepted me. They said I was somebody. They made me feel a part of their family and of something worthwhile."

4. *Deadness of institutional churches.* Cult adherents tend to have three types of church backgrounds.

—Theologically liberal churches, where they never developed a solid faith.

—Status-climbing congregations, only a step removed from country clubs, where they rebelled against sham.

—Conservative Bible-teaching churches, where they learned doctrine but never experienced spiritual closeness and joy.

Speaking to fellow conservatives, Dr. Irvine Robertson of the Moody Bible Institute, observed: "Our strong emphasis . . . on exactness of doctrine may well have overshadowed any emphasis on personal love for Christ or on the indwelling power of the Holy Spirit. This lack of warm, personal love for Christ may, in turn, have opened the door to the . . . mystical, the occult, the esoteric, the unseen."

"Young people today . need some sense of mysticism in their lives," adds William Petersen, editor of *Eternity*.

Never before in history has so much been logically and rationally explained. Even religion itself has lost its mystery. To many people God doesn't answer prayer. Instead, you answer your own prayers. God is no longer worshiped; He is studied. Churches today are filled with study groups, but the celebration and delight of the early Church is missing. . . . We have squeezed out the mysticism and pumped them full of rationalism.

So what is the answer? Jesus Christ alone is the Way, the Truth and the Life. In Him "dwelleth all the fullness of the Godhead bodily" and we are complete in Him. . . . Our lives need to demonstrate that Jesus Christ lives, that He is near, that He satisfies, that He makes our present joyful and our future secure.

Furthermore, dead churches, liberal or conservative, present no challenge to itchy, impatient, idealistic youth. Many offer no more than Gloria Dei Lutheran Church of Huntington Valley, Pennsylvania does in its new Center for Creative and Performing Arts. There young people can study foliage and flowering house plants; beginning flute, clarinet and saxophone; belly dancing; basic astrology; and psychic development which includes self-healing, psychokinesis, psychometry, and telepathy.

"Part of Moon's success," says Brian N. Wills in the *Alliance Witness,* "has been his ability to convince youth that he will solve the world's problems."

There are many churches, of course, where youth are loved, accepted, and challenged with solid truth. But too many other congregations either neglect or underestimate the potential of their young people.

Adults tend to forget that Alexander the Great was only 21 when he conquered the Balkans, 22 when he crossed the Hellespont, and 24 when he built the city of Alexandria; that Ivan the Terrible was 17 when he won the Czar's crown; that Joan of Arc was 17 when her army captured Orleans; that Jesus' Twelve Apostles probably ranged in age from the late teens to early 20s.

Cultists such as Moon and Moses Berg have not forgotten. Nor have the Eastern teachers who are sweeping up drifting, emotionally insecure youths by the thousands.

Despite these tragedies, the cults which are causing so much commotion may in the long run serve to the advantage of our families and institutions.

They will, if they mobilize us to mend the widening moral and spiritual holes in our national fabric.

In Appreciation

In my research I tried diligently to gather all the primary materials available on the religious groups presented in this book. In some instances I went directly to their headquarters. I wanted to be fair and present their sides of controversies. I thank those who provided public relations material.

My best resources were organizations that have arisen in response to cultic activity. They provide training manuals and other authentic material never given out by cults. In particular I thank representatives of the following information groups: Citizens Organized for Public Awareness of Cults, Greensboro, North Carolina; Citizens' Freedom Foundation, Chula Vista, California; Christians United for Jesus as Lord, New York City; Spiritual Counterfeits Project, Berkeley; Christian Apologetics: Research and Information Service, Santa Ana, California; The Christian Research Institute, San Juan Capistrano, California; and Educational Research Analysts, Longview, Texas. Addresses of these and other resources for study of cults are listed in the appendix.

The scores of individuals who shared personal experiences include present and former members of cults and parents who have been directly involved through their children. Interviews ranged from one minute with a tired gum-peddling Moon girl in Chicago to six hours with Andy, an elder in the Children of God for almost six years, in Fresno. I thank them all.

Journalistic colleagues were liberal with insights and research material, especially Alice Murray, religion editor of the *Atlanta Constitution;* Russell Chandler, religion writer of the *Los Angeles Times;* and Edward Plowman, news editor of *Christianity Today.* I am indebted to them beyond measure.

Other individuals whom I must thank are Philip C. Brewer, a California marriage, family, and child counselor, who was a generous host for interviews with former members of the Children of God; Dr. D. Ross Campbell, child psychiatrist, Chattanooga, Tennessee; and George Sheridan, eastern regional director for Interfaith Ministries of the Home Mission Board of the Southern Baptist Convention.

Finally, I thank Marti, my companion in marriage and my colleague in writing, for her editing skills, and Mrs. Jane Wilson for so capably transcribing tapes and typing the final manuscript.

Without the help of these and others this study of recent cults could not have been accomplished. They deserve much credit for helping but none of the blame for unintentional errors I may have made.

James C. Hefley

Appendix

For information or assistance with problems relating to cults discussed in this book, readers may wish to write to:

Spiritual Counterfeits Project, P. O. Box 4308, Berkeley, California 94704.

The Christian Research Institute, Box 500, San Juan Capistrano, California 92675.

Christians United for Jesus as Lord, c/o Calvary Baptist Church, 123 West 57th Street, New York, N. Y. 10019.

Citizens Freedom Foundation, P. O. Box 256, Chula Vista, California 92012.

Citizens Organized for Public Awareness of Cults, P. O. Box 3194, Greensboro, N. C. 27402.

Citizens Engaged in Freeing Minds (Ad hoc national coordinating committee), P. O. Box 5084, Arlington, Texas 76011.

Christian Apologetics: Research and Information Service, P. O. Box 1783, Santa Ana, California 92702.

Educational Research Analysts, Mel and Norma Gabler, P. O. Box 7518, Longview, Texas 75601 (provide reviews of public school curriculums).